Machine Learning for Mobile

Practical guide to building intelligent mobile applications
powered by machine learning

Revathi Gopalakrishnan
Avinash Venkateswarlu

BIRMINGHAM - MUMBAI

Machine Learning for Mobile

Commissioning Editor: Pravin Dhandre
Acquisition Editor: Dayne Castelino
Content Development Editor: Karan Thakkar
Technical Editor: Sagar Sawant
Copy Editor: Safis Editing
Project Coordinator: Namrata Swetta
Proofreader: Safis Editing
Indexer: Rekha Nair
Graphics: Jisha Chirayil
Production Coordinator: Aparna Bhagat

First published: December 2018

Production reference: 1271218

Published by Packt Publishing Ltd.
Livery Place
35 Livery Street
Birmingham
B3 2PB, UK.

ISBN 978-1-78862-935-5

www.packtpub.com

`mapt.io`

Mapt is an online digital library that gives you full access to over 5,000 books and videos, as well as industry leading tools to help you plan your personal development and advance your career. For more information, please visit our website.

Why subscribe?

- Spend less time learning and more time coding with practical eBooks and videos from over 4,000 industry professionals

- Improve your learning with Skill Plans built especially for you

- Get a free eBook or video every month

- Mapt is fully searchable

- Copy and paste, print, and bookmark content

Packt.com

Did you know that Packt offers eBook versions of every book published, with PDF and ePub files available? You can upgrade to the eBook version at `www.packt.com` and as a print book customer, you are entitled to a discount on the eBook copy. Get in touch with us at `customercare@packtpub.com` for more details.

At `www.packt.com`, you can also read a collection of free technical articles, sign up for a range of free newsletters, and receive exclusive discounts and offers on Packt books and eBooks.

Contributors

About the authors

Revathi Gopalakrishnan is a software professional with more than 17 years of experience in the IT industry. She has worked extensively in mobile application development and has played various roles, including developer and architect, and has led various enterprise mobile enablement initiatives for large organizations. She has also worked on a host of consumer applications for various customers around the globe. She has an interest in emerging areas, and machine learning is one of them. Through this book, she has tried to bring out how machine learning can make mobile application development more interesting and super cool. Revathi resides in Chennai and enjoys her weekends with her husband and her two lovely daughters.

Many thanks to the people who helped me complete this book. Thanks to Varsha, Karan, and the Packt team for the wonderful opportunity. Thanks to my parents, husband, and children for all their support. My special thanks to Avinash Venkateswarlu for all his contributions to this book. Heartfelt thanks to the Almighty for his blessing, always.

Avinash Venkateswarlu has more than 3 years' experience in IT and is currently exploring mobile machine learning. He has worked in enterprise mobile enablement projects and is interested in emerging technologies such as mobile machine learning and cryptocurrency. Venkateswarlu works in Chennai, but enjoys spending his weekends in his home town, Nellore. He likes to do farming or yoga when he is not in front of his laptop exploring emerging technologies.

About the reviewer

Karthikeyan NG is the head of engineering and technology at an Indian lifestyle and fashion retail brand. He served as a software engineer at Symantec Corporation, and has worked with two US-based start-ups as an early employee and has built various products. He has more than 9 years of experience with various scalable products using web, mobile, ML, AR, and VR technologies. He is an aspiring entrepreneur and technology evangelist. His interests lie in using new technologies and innovative ideas to resolve problems. He has also bagged prizes from more than 15 hackathons and is a TEDx speaker and a speaker at technology conferences and meetups, as well as a guest lecturer at a Bengaluru University. When not at work, he is found trekking.

Packt is searching for authors like you

If you're interested in becoming an author for Packt, please visit authors.packtpub.com and apply today. We have worked with thousands of developers and tech professionals, just like you, to help them share their insight with the global tech community. You can make a general application, apply for a specific hot topic that we are recruiting an author for, or submit your own idea.

Table of Contents

Preface

This book will help you perform machine learning on mobile with simple practical examples. You start from the basics of machine learning, and by the time you complete the book, you will have a good grasp of what mobile machine learning is and what tools/SDKs are available for implementing mobile machine learning, and will also be able to implement various machine learning algorithms in mobile applications that can be run in both iOS and Android.

You will learn what machine learning is and will understand what is driving mobile machine learning and how it is unique. You will be exposed to all the mobile machine learning tools and SDKs: TensorFlow Lite, Core ML, ML Kit, and Fritz on Android and iOS. This book will explore the high-level architecture and components of each toolkit. By the end of the book, you will have a broad understanding of machine learning models and will be able to perform on-device machine learning. You will get deep-dive insights into machine learning algorithms such as regression, classification, linear **support vector machine** (**SVM**), and random forest. You will learn how to do natural language processing and implement spam message detection. You will learn how to convert existing models created using Core ML and TensorFlow into Fritz models. You will also be exposed to neural networks. You will also get sneak peek into the future of machine learning, and the book also contains an FAQ section to answer all your queries on mobile machine learning. It will help you to build an interesting diet application that provides the calorie values of food items that are captured on a camera, which runs both in iOS and Android.

Who this book is for

Machine Learning for Mobile is for you if you are a mobile developer or machine learning user who aspires to exploit machine learning and use it on mobiles and smart devices. Basic knowledge of machine learning and entry-level experience with mobile application development is preferred.

What this book covers

Chapter 1, *Introduction to Machine Learning on Mobile*, explains what machine learning is and why we should use it on mobile devices. It introduces different approaches to machine learning and their pro and cons.

Chapter 2, *Supervised and Unsupervised Learning Algorithms*, covers supervised and unsupervised approaches of machine learning algorithms. We will also learn about different algorithms, such as Naive Bayes, decision trees, SVM, clustering, associated mapping, and many more.

Chapter 3, *Random Forest on iOS*, covers random forests and decision trees in depth and explains how to apply them to solve machine learning problems. We will also create an application using a decision tree to diagnose breast cancer.

Chapter 4, *TensorFlow Mobile in Android*, introduces TensorFlow for mobile. We will also learn about the architecture of a mobile machine learning application and write an application using TensorFlow in Android.

Chapter 5, *Regression Using Core ML in iOS*, explores regression and Core ML and shows how to apply it to solve a machine learning problem. We will be creating an application using scikit-learn to predict house prices.

Chapter 6, *ML Kit SDK*, explores ML Kit and its benefits. We will be creating some image labeling applications using ML Kit and device and cloud APIs.

Chapter 7, *Spam Message Detection in iOS - Core ML*, introduces natural language processing and the SVM algorithm. We will solve a problem of bulk SMS, that is, whether messages are spam or not.

Chapter 8, *Fritz*, introduces the Fritz mobile machine learning platform. We will create an application using Fritz and Core ML in iOS. We will also see how Fritz can be used with the sample dataset we create earlier in the book.

Chapter 9, *Neural Networks on Mobile*, covers the concepts of neural networks, Keras, and their applications in the field of mobile machine learning. We will be creating an application to recognize handwritten digits and also the TensorFlow image recognition model.

Chapter 10, *Mobile Application Using Google Cloud Vision*, introduces the Google Cloud Vision label-detection technique in an Android application to determine what is in pictures taken by a camera.

Chapter 11, *Future of ML on Mobile Applications*, covers the key features of mobile applications and the opportunities they provide for stakeholders.

Appendix, *Question and Answers*, contains questions that may be on your mind and tries to provide answers to those questions.

To get the most out of this book

Readers need to have prior knowledge of machine learning, Android Studio, and Xcode.

Download the example code files

You can download the example code files for this book from your account at www.packt.com. If you purchased this book elsewhere, you can visit www.packt.com/support and register to have the files emailed directly to you.

You can download the code files by following these steps:

1. Log in or register at www.packt.com.
2. Select the **SUPPORT** tab.
3. Click on **Code Downloads & Errata**.
4. Enter the name of the book in the **Search** box and follow the onscreen instructions.

Once the file is downloaded, please make sure that you unzip or extract the folder using the latest version of:

- WinRAR/7-Zip for Windows
- Zipeg/iZip/UnRarX for Mac
- 7-Zip/PeaZip for Linux

The code bundle for the book is also hosted on GitHub at https://github.com/PacktPublishing/Machine-Learning-for-Mobile. In case there's an update to the code, it will be updated on the existing GitHub repository.

We also have other code bundles from our rich catalog of books and videos available at https://github.com/PacktPublishing/. Check them out!

Download the color images

We also provide a PDF file that has color images of the screenshots/diagrams used in this book. You can download it here: http://www.packtpub.com/sites/default/files/downloads/9781788629355_ColorImages.pdf.

Conventions used

There are a number of text conventions used throughout this book.

CodeInText: Indicates code words in text, database table names, folder names, filenames, file extensions, pathnames, dummy URLs, user input, and Twitter handles. Here is an example: "Now you can take the generated SpamMessageClassifier.mlmodel file and use this in your Xcode."

A block of code is set as follows:

```
# importing required packages
import numpy as np
import pandas as pd
```

When we wish to draw your attention to a particular part of a code block, the relevant lines or items are set in bold:

```
# Reading in and parsing data
raw_data = open('SMSSpamCollection.txt', 'r')
sms_data = []
for line in raw_data:
    split_line = line.split("\t")
    sms_data.append(split_line)
```

Any command-line input or output is written as follows:

```
pip install scikit-learn
pip install numpy
pip install coremltools
pip install pandas
```

Bold: Indicates a new term, an important word, or words that you see onscreen. For example, words in menus or dialog boxes appear in the text like this. Here is an example: "Select **System info** from the **Administration** panel."

Warnings or important notes appear like this.

 Tips and tricks appear like this.

Get in touch

Feedback from our readers is always welcome.

General feedback: If you have questions about any aspect of this book, mention the book title in the subject of your message and email us at customercare@packtpub.com.

Errata: Although we have taken every care to ensure the accuracy of our content, mistakes do happen. If you have found a mistake in this book, we would be grateful if you would report this to us. Please visit www.packt.com/submit-errata, selecting your book, clicking on the Errata Submission Form link, and entering the details.

Piracy: If you come across any illegal copies of our works in any form on the Internet, we would be grateful if you would provide us with the location address or website name. Please contact us at copyright@packt.com with a link to the material.

If you are interested in becoming an author: If there is a topic that you have expertise in and you are interested in either writing or contributing to a book, please visit authors.packtpub.com.

Reviews

Please leave a review. Once you have read and used this book, why not leave a review on the site that you purchased it from? Potential readers can then see and use your unbiased opinion to make purchase decisions, we at Packt can understand what you think about our products, and our authors can see your feedback on their book. Thank you!

For more information about Packt, please visit packt.com.

Introduction to Machine Learning on Mobile

We're living in a world of mobile applications. They've become such a part and parcel of our everyday lives that we rarely look into the numbers behind them. (These include the revenue they make, the actual market size of the business, and the quantitative figures that would fuel the growth of mobile applications.) Let's take a peek at the numbers:

- Forbes predicts that mobile application revenue is slated to hit $189 billion by the year 2020
- We are also seeing that the global smartphone installation base is increasing exponentially. Therefore, the revenue from applications getting installed on them is also increasing at an unimaginable rate

Mobile devices and services are now the hubs for people's entertainment and business lives, as well as for communication. The smartphone has replaced the PC as the most important smart connected device. Mobile innovations, new business models, and mobile technologies are transforming every walk of human life.

Now, we come to machine learning. Why has machine learning been booming recently? Machine learning is not a new subject. It existed over 10-20 years ago, so why is it in focus now and why is everyone talking about it? The reason is simple: data explosion. Social networking and mobile devices have enabled the generation of user data like never before. Ten years ago, you didn't have images uploaded to the cloud like you do today because mobile phone penetration then cannot be compared to what it is today. The 4G connection makes it possible even to live stream **video data on-demand (VDO)** now, so it means more data is running all around the world like never before. The next era is predicted to be the era of the **internet of things (IOT)**, where there is going to be more data-sensor-based data.

All this data is valuable only when we can put it to proper use, derive insights that bring value to us, and bring about unseen data patterns that provide new business opportunities. So, for this to happen, machine learning is the right tool to unlock the stored value in these piles and piles of data that are being accumulated each day.

So, it has become obvious that it is a great time to be a mobile application developer and a great time to be a machine learning data scientist. But how cool would it be if we were able to bring the power of machine learning to mobile devices and develop really cool mobile applications that leverage the power of machine learning? That's what we are trying to do through this book: give insights to mobile application developers on the basics of machine learning, expose them to various machine learning algorithms and mobile machine learning SDKs/tools, and go over developing mobile machine learning applications using these SDKs/tools.

Machine learning in the mobile space is a key innovation area that must be properly understood by mobile developers as it is transforming the way users can visualize and utilize mobile applications. So, how can machine learning transform mobile applications and convert them into applications that are any user's dream? Let me give you some examples to give a bird's eye view of what machine learning can do for mobile applications:

- Facebook and YouTube mobile applications use machine learning—*Recommendations* or *People you might know* are nothing but machine learning in action.
- Apple and Google read the behavior or wording of each user behavior and recommend the next word that is suitable for your style of typing. They have already implemented this in both iOS and Android devices.
- Oval Money analyzes a user's previous transactions and offers them different ways to avoid extra spending.
- Google Maps is using machine learning to make your life easier.
- Django uses machine learning to solve the problem to find a perfect emoji. It is a floating assistant that can be integrated into different messengers.

Machine learning can be applied to mobile applications belonging to any domain—healthcare, finance, games, communication, or anything under the sun. So, let's understand what machine learning is all about.

In this chapter, we will cover the following topics:

- What is machine learning?
- When is it appropriate to go for solutions that get implemented using machine learning?

- Categories of machine learning
- Key algorithms in machine learning
- The process that needs to be followed for implementing machine learning
- Some of the key concepts of machine learning that are good to know
- Challenges in implementing machine learning
- Why use machine learning in mobile applications?
- Ways to implement machine learning in mobile applications

Definition of machine learning

Machine learning is focused on writing software that can learn from past experience. One of the standard definitions of machine learning, as given by Tom Mitchell, a professor at the **Carnegie Mellon University (CMU)**, is the following:

> *A computer program is said to learn from experience E with respect to some class of tasks T and performance measure P, if its performance at tasks in T, as measured by P, improves with experience E.*

For example, a computer program that learns to play chess might improve its performance as measured by its ability to win at the class of tasks involving playing chess, through experience obtained by playing chess against itself. In general, to have a well-defined learning problem, we must identify the class of tasks, the measure of performance to be improved, and the source of experience. Consider that a chess-learning problem consists of the following: task, performance measure, and training experience, where:

- **Task T** is playing chess
- **Performance measure P** is the percentage of games won against opponents
- **Training experience E** is the program playing practice chess games against itself

To put it in simple terms, if a computer program is able to improve the way it performs a task with the help of previous experience, this way you will know the computer has learned. This scenario is very different from one where a program can perform a particular task because its programmers have already defined all the parameters and have provided the data required to do so. A normal program can perform the task of playing chess because the programmers have written the code to play chess with a built-in winning strategy. However, a machine learning program does not possess a built-in strategy; in fact, it only has a set of rules of the legal moves in the game, and what a winning scenario is. In such a case, the program needs to learn by repeatedly playing the game until it can win.

When is it appropriate to go for machine learning systems?

Is machine learning applicable to all scenarios? When exactly should we have the machine learn rather than directly programming the machine with instructions to carry out the task?

Machine learning systems are not knowledge-based systems. In knowledge-based systems, we can directly use the knowledge to codify all possible rules to infer a solution. We go for machine learning when such codification of instructions is not straightforward. Machine learning programs will be more applicable in the following scenarios:

- **Very complex tasks that are difficult to program**: There are regular tasks humans perform, such as speaking, driving, seeing and recognizing things, tasting, and classifying things by looking at them, which seem so simple to us. But, we do not know how our brains are wired or programmed or what rules need to be defined to perform all this seamlessly, for which we could create a program to replicate these actions. It is possible through machine learning to perform some of them, not to the extent that humans do, but machine learning has great potential here.
- **Very complex tasks that deal with a huge volume of data**: There are tasks that include analyzing huge volumes of data and finding hidden patterns, or coming up with new correlations in the data, that are not humanly possible. Machine learning is helpful for tasks for which we do not humanly know the steps to arrive at a solution and which are so complex in nature due to the various solution possibilities that it is not humanly possible to determine solutions.
- **Adapting to changes in environment and data**: A program hardcoded with a set of instructions cannot adapt itself to the changing environment and is not capable of scaling up to new environments. Both of these can be achieved using machine learning programs.

 Machine learning is an art, and a data scientist who specializes in machine learning needs to have a mixture of skills—mathematics, statistics, data analysis, engineering, creative arts, bookkeeping, neuroscience, cognitive science, economics, and so on. He needs to be a jack of all trades and a master of machine learning.

The machine learning process

The machine learning process is an iterative process. It cannot be completed in one go. The most important activities to be performed for a machine learning solution are as follows:

1. Define the machine learning problem (it must be well-defined).
2. Gather, prepare, and enhance the data that is required.
3. Use that data to build a model. This step goes in a loop and covers the following substeps. At times, it may also lead to revisiting *Step 2* on data or even require the redefinition of the problem statement:
    - Select the appropriate model/machine learning algorithm
    - Train the machine learning algorithm on the training data and build the model
    - Test the model
    - Evaluate the results
    - Continue this phase until the evaluation result is satisfactory and finalize the model
4. Use the finalized model to make future predictions for the problem statement.

There are four major steps involved in the whole process, which is iterative and repetitive, till the objective is met. Let's get into the details of each step in the following sections. The following diagram will give a quick overview of the entire process, so it is easy to go into the details:

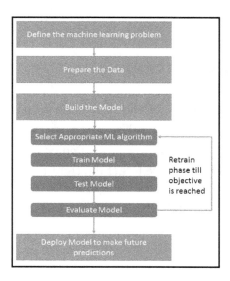

Defining the machine learning problem

As defined by Tom Mitchell, the problem must be a well-defined machine learning problem. The three important questions to be solved at this stage include the following:

- Do we have the right problem?
- Do we have the right data?
- Do we have the right success criteria?

The problem should be such that the outcome that is going to be obtained as a solution to the problem is valuable for the business. There should be sufficient historical data that should be available for learning/training purposes. The objective should be measurable and we should know how much of the objective has been achieved at any point in time.

For example, if we are going to identify fraudulent transactions from a set of online transactions, then determining such fraudulent transactions is definitely valuable for the business. We need to have a sufficient set of online transactions. We should have a sufficient set of transactions that belong to various fraudulent categories. We should also have a mechanism to determine whether the outcome predicted as a fraudulent or nonfraudulent transaction can be verified and validated for the accuracy of prediction.

 To give users an idea of what data would be sufficient to implement machine learning, we could say that a dataset of at least 100 items should be fine for starters and 1,000 would be nice. The more data we have that may cover all realistic scenarios for the problem domain, the better it is for the learning algorithm.

Preparing the data

The data preparation activity is key to the success of the learning solution. The data is the key entity required for machine learning and it must be prepared properly to ensure the proper end results and objectives are obtained.

 Data engineers usually spend around 80-90 percent of their overall time in the data preparation phase to get the right data, as this is fundamental and the most critical task for the success of the implementation of the machine learning program.

The following actions need to be performed in order to prepare the data:

1. **Identify all sources of data**: We need to identify all data sources that can solve the problem at hand and collect the data from multiple sources—files, databases, emails, mobile devices, the internet, and so on.

2. **Explore the data**: This step involves understanding the nature of the data, as follows:
   - Integrate data from different systems and explore it.
   - Understand the characteristics and nature of the data.
   - Go through the correlations between data entities.
   - Identify the outliers. Outliers will help with identifying any problems with the data.
   - Apply various statistical principles such as calculating the median, mean, mode, range, and standard deviation to arrive at data skewness. This will help with understanding the nature and spread of data.
   - If data is skewed or we see the value of the range is outside the expected boundary, we know that the data has a problem and we need to revisit the source of the data.
   - Visualization of data through graphs will also help with understanding the spread and quality of the data.

3. **Preprocess the data**: The goal of this step is to create data in a format that can be used for the next step:
   - **Data cleansing**:
     - Addressing the missing values. A common strategy used to impute missing values is to replace missing values with the mean or median value. It is important to define a strategy for replacing missing values.
     - Addressing duplicate values, invalid data, inconsistent data, outliers, and so on.
   - **Feature selection**: Choosing the data features that are the most appropriate for the problem at hand. Removing redundant or irrelevant features that will simplify the process.
   - **Feature transformation**: This phase maps the data from one format to another that will help in proceeding to the next steps of machine learning. This involves normalizing the data and dimensionality reduction. This involves combining various features into one feature or creating new features. For example, say we have the date and time as attributes.

It would be more meaningful to have them transformed as a day of the week, a day of the month, and a year, which would provide more meaningful insight:

- To create Cartesian products of one variable with another. For example, if we have two variables, such as population density (maths, physics, and commerce) and gender (girls and boys), the features formed by a Cartesian product of these two variables might contain useful information resulting in features such as (`maths_girls`, `physics_girls`, `commerce_girls`, `maths_boys`, `physics_boys`, and `commerce_boys`).

- Binning numeric variables to categories. For example, the size value of hips/shoulders can be binned to categories such as small, medium, large, and extra large.

- Domain-specific features, for example, combining the subjects maths, physics, and chemistry to a maths group and combining physics, chemistry, and biology to a biology group.

4. **Divide the data into training and test sets**: Once the data is transformed, we then need to select the required test set and a training set. An algorithm is evaluated against the test dataset after training it on the training dataset. This split of the data into training and test datasets may be as direct as performing a random split of data (66 percent for training, 34 percent for testing) or it may involve more complicated sampling methods.

The 66 percent/34 percent split is just a guide. If you have 1 million pieces of data, a 90 percent/10 percent split should be enough. With 100 million pieces of data, you can even go down to 99 percent/1 percent.

A trained model is not exposed to the test dataset during training and any predictions made on that dataset are designed to be indicative of the performance of the model in general. As such, we need to make sure the selection of datasets is representative of the problem that we are solving.

Building the model

The model-building phase consists of many substeps, as indicated earlier, such as the selection of an appropriate machine learning algorithm, training the model, testing it, evaluating the model to determine whether the objectives have been achieved, and, if not, entering into the retraining phase by either selecting the same algorithm with different datasets or selecting an entirely new algorithm till the objectives are reached.

Selecting the right machine learning algorithm

The first step toward building the model is to select the right machine learning algorithm that might solve the problem.

This step involves selecting the right machine learning algorithm and building a model, then training it using the training set. The algorithm will learn from the training data patterns that map the variables to the target, and it will output a model that captures these relationships. The machine learning model can then be used to get predictions on new data for which you do not know the target answer.

Training the machine learning model

The goal is to select the most appropriate algorithm for building the machine learning model, training it, and then analyzing the results received. We begin by selecting appropriate machine learning techniques to analyze the data. The next chapter, that is, `Chapter 2`, *Random Forest on iOS*, will talk about the different machine learning algorithms and presents details of the types of problems for which they would be apt.

The training process and analyzing the results also varies based on the algorithms selected for training.

The training phase usually uses all the attributes of data present in the transformed data, which will include the predictor attributes as well as the objective attributes. All the data features are used in the training phase.

Testing the model

Once the machine learning algorithm is trained in the training data, the next step is to run the model in the test data.

The entire set of attributes or features of the data is divided into predictor attributes and objective attributes. The predictor attributes/features of the dataset are fed as input to the machine learning model and the model uses these attributes to predict the objective attributes. The test set uses only the predictor attributes. Now, the algorithm uses the predictor attributes and outputs predictions on objective attributes. Once the output is provided, it is compared against the actual data to understand the quality of output from the algorithm.

The results should be properly presented for further analysis. What to present in the results and how to present them are critical. They may also bring to the fore new business problems.

Evaluation of the model

There should be a process to test machine learning algorithms and discover whether or not we have chosen the right algorithms, and to validate the output the algorithm provides against the problem statement.

This is the last step in the machine learning process, where we check the accuracy with the defined threshold for success criteria and, if the accuracy is greater than or equal to the threshold, then we are done. If not, we need to start all over again with a different machine learning algorithm, different parameter settings, more data, and changed data transformation. All steps in the entire machine learning process can be repeated, or a subset of it can be repeated. These are repeated till we come to the definition of "done" and are satisfied with the results.

 The machine learning process is a very iterative one. Findings from one step may require a previous step to be repeated with new information. For example, during the data transformation step, we may find some data quality issues that may require us to go back to acquire more data from a different source.

Each step may also require several iterations. This is of particular interest, as the data preparation step may undergo several iterations, and the model selection may undergo several iterations. In the entire sequence of activities stated for performing machine learning, any activity can be repeated any number of times. For example, it is common to try different machine learning algorithms to train the model before moving on to testing the model. So, it is important to recognize that this is a highly iterative process and not a linear one.

Test set creation: We have to define the test dataset clearly. The goal of the test dataset is as follows:

- Quickly and consistently test the algorithm that has been selected to solve the problem
- Test a variety of algorithms to determine whether they are able to solve the problem
- Determine which algorithm would be worth using to solve the problem
- Determine whether there is a problem with the data considered for evaluation purposes as, if all algorithms consistently fail to produce proper results, there is a possibility that the data itself might require a revisit

Performance measure: The performance measure is a way to evaluate the model created. Different performance metrics will need to be used to evaluate different machine learning models. These are standard performance measures from which we can choose to test our model. There may not be a need to customize the performance measures for our model.

The following are some of the important terms that need to be known to understand the performance measure of algorithms:

- **Overfitting**: The machine learning model is overfitting the training data when we see that the model performs well on the training data but does not perform well on the evaluation data. This is because the model is memorizing the data it has seen and is unable to generalize to unseen examples.
- **Underfitting**: The machine learning model is underfitting the training data when the model performs poorly on the training data. This is because the model is unable to capture the relationship between the input examples (often called **X**) and the target values (often called **Y**).
- **Cross-validation**: Cross-validation is a technique to evaluate predictive models by partitioning the original sample into a training set to train the model, and a test set to evaluate it. In k-fold cross-validation, the original sample is randomly partitioned into *k* equally sized subsamples.
- **Confusion matrix**: In the field of machine learning, and specifically the problem of statistical classification, a confusion matrix, also known as an **error matrix**, is a specific table layout that allows visualization of the performance of an algorithm.
- **Bias**: Bias is the tendency of a model to make predictions in a consistent way.
- **Variance**: Variance is the tendency of a model to make predictions that vary from the true relationship between the parameters and the labels.
- **Accuracy**: Correct results are divided by total results.
- **Error**: Incorrect results are divided by total results.

- **Precision**: The number of correct results returned by a machine learning algorithm are divided by the number of all returned results.
- **Recall**: The number of correct results returned by a machine learning algorithm are divided by the number of results that should have been returned.

Making predictions/Deploying in the field

Once the model is ready, it can be deployed to the field for usage. Predictions can be done on the upcoming dataset using the model that has been built and deployed in the field.

Types of learning

There some variations in how to define the types of machine learning algorithms. The most common categorization of algorithms is done based on the learner type of the algorithm and is categorized as follows:

- Supervised learning
- Unsupervised learning
- Semi-supervised learning
- Reinforcement learning

Supervised learning

Supervised learning is a type of learning where the model is fed with enough information and knowledge and closely supervised to learn, so that, based on the learning it has done, it can predict the outcome for a new dataset.

Here, the model is trained in supervision mode, similar to supervision by teachers, where we feed the model with enough training data containing the input/predictors and train it and show the correct answers or output. So, based on this, it learns and will become capable of predicting the output for unseen data that may come in the future.

A classic example of this would be the standard Iris dataset. The Iris dataset consists of three species of iris and for each species, the sepal length, sepal width, petal length, and petal width is given. And for a specific pattern of the four parameters, the label is provided as to what species such a set should belong to. With this learning in place, the model will be able to predict the label—in this case, the iris species, based on the feature set—in this case, the four parameters.

Supervised learning algorithms try to model relationships and dependencies between the target prediction output and the input features such that we can predict the output values for new data based on those relationships which it learned from the previous datasets.

The following diagram will give you an idea of what supervised learning is. The data with labels is given as input to build the model through supervised learning algorithms. This is the training phase. Then the model is used to predict the class label for any input data without the label. This is the testing phase:

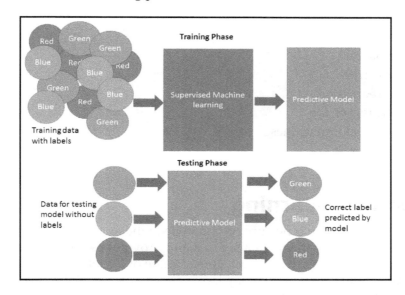

Again, in supervised learning algorithms, the predicted output could be a discrete/categorical value or it could be a continuous value based on the type of scenario considered and the dataset taken into consideration. If the output predicted is a discrete/categorical value, such algorithms fall under the classification algorithms, and if the output predicted is a continuous value, such algorithms fall under the regression algorithms.

If there is a set of emails and you want to learn from them and be able to tell which emails belong to the spam category and which emails belong to the non-spam category, then the algorithm to be used for this purpose will be a supervised learning algorithm belonging to the classification type. Here, you need to feed the model with a set of emails and feed enough knowledge to the model about the attributes, based on which it would segregate the email to either the spam category or the non-spam category. So the predicted output would be a categorical value, that is, spam or non-spam.

Let's take the use case where based on a given set of parameters, we need to predict what would be the price of a house in a given area. This cannot be a categorical value. It is going to be a range or a continuous value and also be subject to change on a regular basis. In this problem, the model also needs to be provided with sufficient knowledge, based on which it is going to predict the pricing value. This type of algorithm belongs to the supervised learning regression category of algorithms.

There are various algorithms belonging to the supervised category of the machine learning family:

- K-nearest neighbors
- Naive Bayes
- Decision trees
- Linear regression
- Logistic regression
- Support vector machines
- Random forest

Unsupervised learning

In this learning pattern, there is no supervision done to the model to make it learn. The model learns by itself based on the data fed to it and provides us with patterns it has learned. It doesn't predict any discrete categorical value or a continuous value, but rather provides the patterns it has understood by looking at the data fed into it. The training data fed in is unlabeled and doesn't provide sufficient knowledge information for the model to learn.

Here, there's no supervision at all; actually, the model might be able to teach us new things after it learns the data. These algorithms are very useful where a feature set is too large and the human user doesn't know what to look for in the data.

This class of algorithms is mainly used for **pattern detection** and **descriptive modeling**. Descriptive modeling summarizes the relevant information from the data and presents a summary of what has already occurred, whereas predictive modeling summarizes the data and presents a summary of what can occur.

Unsupervised learning algorithms can be used for both categories of prediction. They use the input data to come up with different patterns, a summary of the data points, and insights that are not visible to human eyes. They come up with meaningful derived data or patterns of data that are helpful for end users.

The following diagram will give you an idea of what unsupervised learning is. The data without labels is given as input to build the model through unsupervised learning algorithms. This is the **Training Phase**. Then the model is used to predict the proper patterns for any input data without the label. This is the **Testing Phase**:

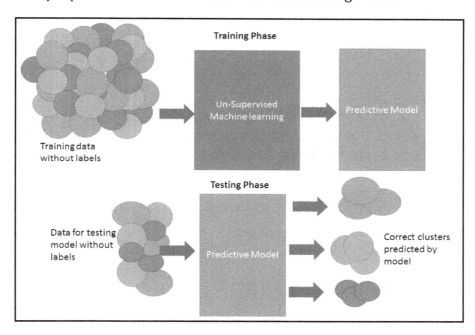

In this family of algorithms, which is also based on the input data fed to the model and the method adopted by the model to infer patterns in the dataset, there emerge two common categories of algorithms. These are clustering and association rule mapping algorithms.

Clustering is the model that analyzes the input dataset and groups data items with similarity into the same cluster. It produces different clusters and each cluster will hold data items that are more similar to each other than in items belonging to other clusters. There are various mechanisms that can be used to create these clusters.

Customer segmentation is one example for clustering. We have a huge dataset of customers and capture all features of customers. The model could come up with interesting cluster patterns of customers that may be very obvious to the human eye. Such clusters could be very helpful for targeted campaigns and marketing.

On the other hand, association rule learning is a model to discover relations between variables in large datasets. A classic example would be market basket analysis. Here, the model tries to find strong relationships between different items in the market basket. It predicts relationships between items and determines how likely or unlikely it is for a user to purchase a particular item when they also purchase another item. For example, it might predict that a user who purchases bread will also purchase milk, or a user who purchases wine will also purchase diapers, and so on.

The algorithms belonging to this category include the following:

- Clustering algorithms:
  - Centroid-based algorithms
  - Connectivity-based algorithms
  - Density-based algorithms
  - Probabilistic
  - Dimensionality reduction
  - Neural networks/deep learning
- Association rule learning algorithm

Semi-supervised learning

In the previous two types, either there are no labels for all the observations in the dataset or labels are present for all the observations. Semi-supervised learning falls in between these two. In many practical situations, the cost of labeling is quite high, since it requires skilled human experts to do that. So, if labels are absent in the majority of the observations, but present in a few, then semi-supervised algorithms are the best candidates for the model building.

Speech analysis is one example of a semi-supervised learning model. Labeling audio files is very costly and requires a very high level of human effort. Applying semi-supervised learning models can really help to improve traditional speech analytic models.

In this class of algorithms, also based on the output predicted, which may be categorical or continuous, the algorithm family could be regression or classification.

Reinforcement learning

Reinforcement learning is goal-oriented learning based on interactions with the environment. A reinforcement learning algorithm (called the **agent**) continuously learns from the environment in an iterative fashion. In the process, the agent learns from its experiences of the environment until it explores the full range of possible states and is able to reach the target state.

Let's take the example of a child learning to ride a bicycle. The child tries to learn by riding it, it may fall, it will understand how to balance, how to continue the flow without falling, how to sit in the proper position so that weight is not moved to one side, studies the surface, and also plans actions as per the surface, slope, hill, and so on. So, it will learn all possible scenarios and states required to learn to ride the bicycle. A fall may be considered as negative feedback and the ability to ride along stride may be a positive reward for the child. This is classic reinforcement learning. This is the same as what the model does to determine the ideal behavior within a specific context, in order to maximize its performance. Simple reward feedback is required for the agent to learn its behavior; this is known as the **reinforcement signal**:

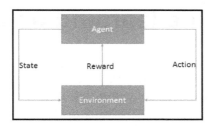

Now, we will just summarize the type of learning algorithms we have seen through a diagram, so that it will be handy and a reference point for you to decide on choosing the algorithm for a given problem statement:

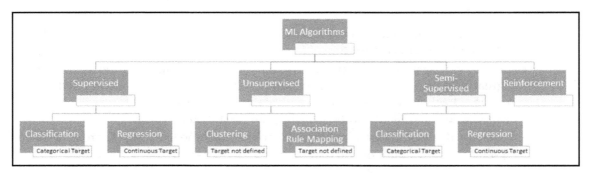

Challenges in machine learning

Some of the challenges we face in machine learning are as follows:

- Lack of a well-defined machine learning problem. If the problem is not defined clearly as per the definition with required criteria, the machine learning problem is likely to fail.
- Feature engineering. This relates to every activity with respect to data and its features that are essential for the success of the machine learning problem.
- No clarity between the training set and test set. Often the model performs well in the training phase, but fails miserably in the field due to a lack of all possible data in the training set. This should be taken care of for the model to succeed in the field.
- The right choice of algorithm. There is a wide range of algorithms available, but which one suits our problem best? This should be chosen properly in the iteration with proper parameters required.

Why use machine learning on mobile devices?

Machine learning is needed to extract meaningful and actionable information from huge amounts of data. A significant amount of computation is required to analyze huge amounts of data and arrive at an inference. This processing is ideal for a cloud environment. However, if we could carry out machine learning on a mobile, the following would be the advantages:

- Machine learning could be performed offline, as there would be no need to send all the data that the mobile has to the network and wait for results back from the server.
- The network bandwidth cost incurred, if any, due to the transmission of mobile data to the server is avoided.
- Latency can be avoided by processing data locally. Mobile machine learning has a great deal of responsiveness as we don't have to wait for connection and response back from the server. It might take up to 1-2 seconds for server response, but mobile machine learning can do it instantly.
- Privacy—this is another advantage of mobile machine learning. There is no need to send the user data outside the mobile device, enabling better privacy.

Machine learning started in computers, but the emerging trend shows that mobile app development with machine learning implemented on mobile devices is the next big thing. Modern mobile devices show the high productive capacity level that is enough to perform appropriate tasks to the same degree as traditional computers do. Also, there are some signals from global corporations that confirm this assumption:

- Google launched TensorFlow for Mobile. There is very significant interest from the developer community also.
- Apple has launched Siri SDK and Core ML and now all developers can incorporate this feature into their apps.
- Lenovo is working on their new smartphone that also performs without an internet connection and executes indoor geolocation and augmented reality.
- There is significant research being undertaken by most of the mobile chip makers, whether it is Apple, Qualcomm, Samsung, or even Google itself, working on hardware dedicated to speeding up machine learning on mobile devices.
- There are many innovations happening in the hardware layer to enable hardware acceleration, which would make machine learning on mobile easy.
- Many mobile-optimized models such as MobileNets, Squeeze Net, and so on have been open sourced.
- The availability of IoT devices and smart hardware appliances is increasing, which will aid in innovation.
- There are more use cases that people are interested in for offline scenarios.
- There is more and more focus on user data privacy and users' desire for their personal data not to leave their mobile devices at all.

Some classic examples of machine learning on mobile devices are as follows:

- Speech recognition
- Computer vision and image classification
- Gesture recognition
- Translation from one language into another
- Interactive on-device detection of text
- Autonomous vehicles, drone navigation, and robotics
- Patient-monitoring systems and mobile applications interacting with medical devices

Ways to implement machine learning in mobile applications

Now, we clearly understand what machine learning is and what the key tasks to be performed in a learning problem are. The four main activities to be performed for any machine learning problem are as follows:

1. Define the machine learning problem
2. Gather the data required
3. Use that data to build/train a model
4. Use the model to make predictions

Training the model is the most difficult part of the whole process. Once we have trained the model and have the model ready, using it to infer or predict for a new dataset is very easy.

For all the four steps provided in the preceding points, we clearly need to decide where we intend to use them—on a device or in the cloud.

The main things we need to decide are as follows:

- First of all, are we going to train and create a custom model or use a prebuilt model?
- If we want to train our own model, do we do this training on our desktop machine or in the cloud? Is there a possibility to train the model on a mobile device?
- Once the model is available, are we going to put it in a local device and do the inference on the device or are we going to deploy the model in the cloud and do the inference from there?

The following are the broad possibilities to implement machine learning in mobile applications. We will get into the details of it in the upcoming sections:

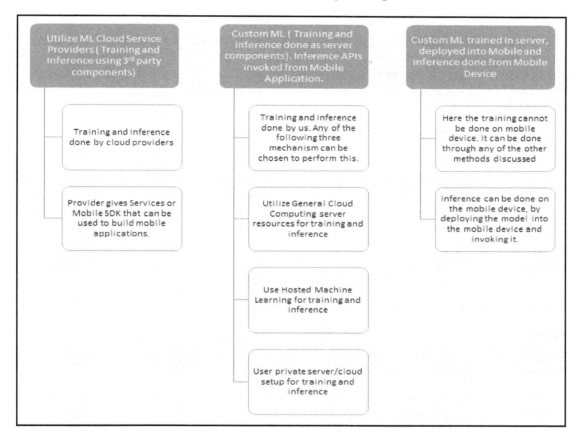

Utilizing machine learning service providers for a machine learning model

There are many service providers offering machine learning as a service. We can just utilize them.

Examples of such providers who provide machine learning as a service are listed in the following points. This list is increasing every day:

- Clarifai
- Google Cloud Vision

- Microsoft Azure Cognitive Services
- IBM Watson
- Amazon Web Services

If we were to go with this model, the training is already done, the model is built, and model features are exposed as web services. So, all we have to do from the mobile application is simply to invoke the model service with the required dataset and get the results from the cloud provider and then display the results in the mobile application as per our requirement:

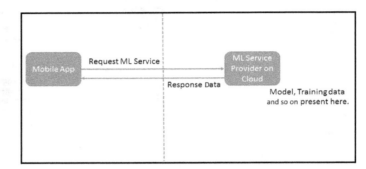

Some of the providers provide an SDK that makes the integration work very simple.

There may be a charge that we need to provide to the cloud service provider for utilizing their machine learning web services. There may be various models based on which this fee is charged, for example, the number of times it is invoked, the type of model, and so on.

So, this is a very simple way to use machine learning services, without actually having to do anything about the model. On top of this, the machine learning service provider keeps the model updated by constant retraining, including new datasets whenever required, and so on. So, the maintenance and improvement of the model is automatically taken care of on a routine basis.

So, this type of model is easy for people who are experts in mobile but don't know anything about ML, but want to build an ML-enabled app.

So the obvious benefits of such a cloud-based machine learning service are as follows:

- It is easy to use.
- No knowledge of machine learning is required and the tough part of the training is done by the service provider.

- Retraining, model updates, support, and maintenance of the model are done by the provider.
- Charges are paid only as per usage. There is no overhead to maintain the model, the data for training, and so on.

Some of the flip sides of this approach are as follows:

- The prediction will be done in the cloud. So, the dataset for which the prediction or inference is to be done has to be sent to the cloud. The dataset has to be maintained at the optimal size.
- Since data moves over the network, there may be some performance issues experienced in the app, since the whole thing now becomes network-dependent.
- Mobile applications won't work in offline mode and work as completely online applications.
- Mostly, charges are to be paid per request. So, if the number of users of the application increases exponentially, the cost for the machine learning service also increases.
- The training and retraining is in the control of the cloud service provider. So, they might have done training for common datasets. If our mobile application is going to use something really unique, chances are that the predictions may not work.

To get started with ML-enabled mobile applications, the model is the right fit both with respect to cost and technical feasibility. And absolutely fine for a machine learning newbie.

Ways to train the machine learning model

There are various ways to go about training our own machine learning model. Before getting into ways to train our model, why would we go for training our own model?

Mostly, if our data is special or unique in some way and very much specific to our requirements and when the existing solutions cannot be used to solve our problem, we may decide to train our own model.

For training our own model, a good dataset is required. A good dataset is one which is qualitatively and quantitatively good and large.

Training our model can be done in multiple ways/places based on our requirements and the amount of data:

- **On a desktop (training in the cloud)**:
  - General cloud computing
  - Hosted machine learning
  - Private cloud/simple server machine
- **On a device**: This is not very feasible. We can only deploy the trained model on a mobile device and invoke it from a mobile device. So far, the training process itself is not feasible from a mobile device.

On a desktop (training in the cloud)

If we have decided to carry out the training process on a desktop, we have to do it in the cloud or on our humble local server, based on our needs.

If we decide to use the cloud, again we have the following two options:

- Generic cloud computing
- Hosted machine learning

Generic cloud computing is similar to utilizing the cloud service provider to carry out our work. We want to carry out machine learning training. So, in order to carry this out, whatever is required, say hardware, storage, and so on, must be obtained from them. We can do whatever we need with these resources. We need to place our training dataset here, run the training logic/algorithms, build the model, and so on.

Once the training is done and the model is created, the model can be taken anywhere for usage. To the cloud provider, we pay the charges for utilizing the hardware and storage only.

Amazon Web Services (**AWS**) and Azure are some of the cloud-computing vendors.

The benefits of using this approach are as follows:

- The hardware/storage can be procured and used on the go. There is no need to worry about increasing storage and so on, when the amount of training data increases. It can be incremented when needed by paying the charges.
- Once the training is done and the model is created, we can release the computing resources. Costs incurred on computing resources are only for the training period and hence if we are able to finish the training quickly, we save a lot.
- We are free to download the trained model and use it anywhere.

What we need to be careful about when we go for this approach is the following:

- We need to take care of the entire training work and the model creation. We are only going to use the compute resources required to carry out this work.
- So, we need to know how to train and build the model.

Several companies, such as Amazon, Microsoft, and Google, now offer machine learning as a service on top of their existing cloud services. In the hosted machine learning model, we neither need to worry about the compute resources nor the machine learning models. We need to upload the data for our problem set, choose the model that we want to train for our data from the available list of models, and that's all. The machine learning services take care of training the model and providing the trained model to us for usage.

This approach works really well when we are not so well-versed to write our own custom model and train it, but also do not want to go completely to a machine learning provider to use their service, but want to do something in between. We can choose between the models, upload our unique dataset, and then train it for our requirements.

In this type of approach, the provider usually makes us tied to their platform. We may not be able to download the model and deploy it anywhere else for usage. We may need to be tied to them and utilize their platform from our app for using the trained model.

One more thing to note is that if at a later point in time, we decide to move to another provider, the trained model cannot be exported and imported to the other provider. We may need to carry out the training process again on the new provider platform.

In this approach, we might need to pay for the compute resources –hardware/storage –plus, after the training, to use the trained model, we may need to pay on an ongoing per-usage basis, that is, an on-demand basis; whenever we use it, we need to pay for what we use.

The benefits of using this approach are as follows:

- There is no need to worry about the compute resources/storage required for training the data.
- There is no need to worry about understanding the details of machine learning models to build and train custom models.
- Just upload the data, choose the model to use for training and that's it. Get the trained model for usage
- There is no need to worry about deploying the model to anywhere for consumption from the mobile application.

What we need to be careful about when we go for this approach is as follows:

- Mostly, we may get tied to their platform after the training process in order to use the model obtained after training. However, there are a few exceptions, such as Google's Cloud platform.
- We may be able to choose only from the models provided by the provider. We can only choose from the available list.
- A trained model from one platform cannot be moved to another platform. So, if we decide to change the platform later, we may need to retain again in their platform.
- We may need to pay for compute resources and also pay on an ongoing basis for usage of the model.

Using our private cloud/simple server is similar to training on the generic cloud, except that we need to manage the compute resources/storage. In this approach, the only thing we miss out on is the flexibility given by generic cloud solution providers that include increasing/decreasing the compute and storage resources, the overhead to maintain and manage these compute resources, and so on.

The major advantage we get with this approach is about the security of the data we get. If we think our data is really unique and needs to be kept completely secured, this is a good approach to use. Here, everything is done in-house using our own resources.

The benefits of using this approach are as follows:

- Absolutely everything is in our control, including the compute resources, training data, model, and so on
- It is more secure

What we need to be careful about when we go for this approach is the following:

- Everything needs to be managed by us
- We should be clear with the machine learning concepts, data, model, and training process
- Continuous availability of compute resources/hardware is to be managed by us
- If our dataset is going to be huge, this might not be very effective, as we may need to scale the compute resources and storage as per the increasing dataset size

On a device

The training process on a device has still not picked up. It may be feasible for a very small dataset. Since the compute resources required to train the data and also the storage required to store the data is more, generally mobile is not the preferred platform to carry out the training process.

The retraining phase also becomes complicated if we use mobile as a platform for the training process.

Ways to carry out the inference – making predictions

Once the model is created, we need to use the model for a new dataset in order to infer or make the predictions. Similar to how we had various ways in which we could carry out the training process, we can have multiple approaches to carry out the inference process also:

- On a server:
    - General cloud computing
    - Hosted machine learning
    - Private cloud/simple server machine
- On a device

Inference on a server would require a network request and the application will need to be online to use this approach. But, inference on the device means the application can be a completely offline application. So, obviously, all the overheads for an online app, in terms of speed/performance, and so on, is better for an offline application.

However, for inference, if there are more compute resources—that is, processing power/memory is required—the inference cannot be done on the device.

Inference on a server

In this approach, once the model is trained, we host the model on a server to utilize it from the application.

The model can be hosted either in a cloud machine or on a local server, or it can be that of a hosted machine learning provider. The server is going to publish the endpoint URL, which needs to be accessed to utilize it to make the required predictions. The required dataset is to be passed as input to the service.

Doing the inference on a server makes the mobile application simple. The model can be improved periodically, without having to redeploy the mobile client application. New features can be added into the model easily. There is no requirement to upgrade the mobile application for any model changes.

The benefits of using this approach are as follows:

- Mobile application becomes relatively simple.
- The model can be updated at any time without the redeployment of the client application.
- It is easy to support multiple OS platforms without writing the complex inference logic in an OS-specific platform. Everything is done in the backend.

What we need to be careful about when we go for this approach is the following:

- The application can work only in online mode. The application has to connect to backend components in order to carry out the inference logic.
- There is a requirement to maintain the server hardware and software and ensure it is up and running. It needs to scale for users. For scalability, the additional cost is required to manage multiple servers and ensure they are up and running always.
- Users need to transmit the data to the backend for inference. If the data is huge, they might experience performance issues as well as users needing to pay for transmitting the data.

Inference on a device

In this approach, the machine learning model is loaded into the client mobile application. To make a prediction, the mobile application runs all the inference computations locally on the device, on its own CPU or GPU. It need not communicate to the server for anything related to machine learning.

Speed is the major reason for doing inference directly on a device. We need not send a request over the server and wait for the reply. Things happen almost instantaneously.

Since the model is bundled along with the mobile application, it is not very easy to upgrade the model in one place and reuse it. The mobile application upgrade has to be done. The upgrade push has to be provided to all active users. All this is a big overhead and will consume a lot of effort and time.

Even for small changes, retraining the model with very few additional parameters will involve a complex process of an application upgrade, pushing the upgrade to live users, and maintaining the required infrastructure for the same.

The benefits of using this approach are as follows:

- Users can use the mobile application in offline mode. Availability of the network is not essential to operate the mobile application.
- The prediction and inference can happen very quickly since the model is right there along with the application source code.
- The data required to predict need not be sent over the network and hence no bandwidth cost is involved for users.
- There is no overhead to run and maintain server infrastructure, and multiple servers can be managed for user scalability.

What we need to be careful about when we go for this approach is the following:

- Since the model is included along with the application, it is difficult to make changes to the model. The changes can be done, but to make the changes reach all client applications is a costly process that consumes effort and time.
- The model file, if huge, can increase the size of the application significantly.
- The prediction logic should be written for each OS platform the application supports, say iOS or Android.
- All of the model has to be properly encrypted or obfuscated to make sure it is not hacked by other developers.

In this book, we are going to look into the details of utilizing the SDKs and tools available to perform tasks related to machine learning locally on a mobile device itself.

Popular mobile machine learning tools and SDKs

The following are the key machine learning SDKs we are going to explore in this book:

- TensorFlow Lite from Google
- Core ML from Apple
- Caffe2Go from Facebook
- ML Kit from Google
- Fritz.ai

We will go over the details of the SDKs and also sample mobile machine learning applications built using these SDKs, leveraging different types of machine learning algorithms.

Skills needed to implement on-device machine learning

In order to implement machine learning on a mobile device, deep knowledge of machine learning algorithms, the entire process, and how to build the machine learning model is not required. For a mobile application developer who knows how to create mobile applications using iOS or Android SDK, just like how they utilize the backend APIs to invoke the backend business logic, they need to know the mechanism to invoke the machine learning models from their mobile application to make predictions. They need to know the mechanism to import the machine learning model into the mobile resources folder and then invoke the various features of the model to make the predictions.

To summarize, the following diagram shows the steps for a mobile developer to implement machine learning on a device:

 Machine learning implementation on mobiles can be considered similar to backend API integration. You build the API separately and then integrate where required. Similarly, you build the model separately outside the device and import it into the mobile application and integrate where required.

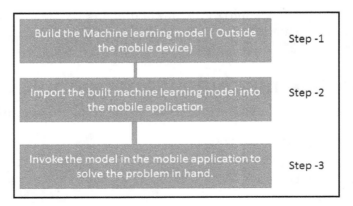

Summary

In this chapter, we were introduced to machine learning, including the types of machine learning, where they are used, and practical scenarios where they can be used. We also saw what a well-defined machine learning problem is and also understood when we need to go for a machine learning solution. Then we saw the machine learning process and the steps involved in building the machine learning model, from defining the problem of deploying the model to the field. We saw certain important terms used in the machine learning namespace that are good to know.

We saw the challenges in implementing machine learning and, specifically, we saw the need for implementing the machine learning in mobiles and the challenges surrounding this. We saw different design approaches for implementing machine learning on mobile applications. We also saw the benefits of using each of the design approaches and also noted the important considerations that we need to analyze and keep in mind when we decide to use each of the solution approaches for implementing machine learning on mobile devices. Lastly, we glanced through the important mobile machine learning SDKs that we are going to go through in detail in subsequent chapters. These include TensorFlow lite, Core ML, Fritz, ML Kit, and lastly, the cloud-based Google Vision.

In the next chapter, we will learn more about Supervised and Unsupervised machine learning and how to implement it for mobiles.

2
Supervised and Unsupervised Learning Algorithms

In the previous chapter, we got some insight into the various aspects of machine learning and were introduced to the various ways in which machine learning algorithms could be categorized. In this chapter, we will go a step further into machine learning algorithms and try to understand supervised and unsupervised learning algorithms. This categorization is based on the learning mechanism of the algorithm, and is the most popular.

In this chapter, we will be covering the following topics:

- An introduction to the supervised learning algorithm in the form of a detailed practical example to help understand it and its guiding principles
- The key supervised learning algorithms and their application areas:
    - Naive Bayes
    - Decision trees
    - Linear regression
    - Logistic regression
    - Support vector machines
    - Random forest
- An introduction to the unsupervised learning algorithm in the form of a detailed practical example to help understand it
- The key unsupervised learning algorithms and their application areas:
    - Clustering algorithms
    - Association rule mapping
- A broad overview of the different mobile SDKs and tools available to implement these algorithms in mobile devices

Introduction to supervised learning algorithms

Let's look at supervised learning for simple day-to-day activities. A parent asks their 15-year-old son to go to the store and get some vegetables. They give him a list of vegetables, say beets, carrots, beans, and tomatoes, that they want him to buy. He goes to the store and is able to identify the list of vegetables as per the list provided by his mother from all the other numerous varieties of vegetables present in the store and put them in his cart before going to the checkout. How was this possible?

Simple. The parent had provided enough training to the son by providing instances of each and every vegetable, which equipped him with sufficient knowledge of the vegetables. The son used the knowledge he has gained to choose the correct vegetables. He used the various attributes of the vegetables to arrive at the correct class label of the vegetable, which, in this case, is the name of the vegetable. The following table gives us a few of the attributes of the vegetables present in the list, by means of which the son was able to recognize the class label, that is, the vegetable name:

Vegetable name = class label	Carrots	Beets	Beans	Tomatoes
Attribute 1 = Color	Orange	Pink	Green	Red
Attribute 2 = Shape	Cone	Round	Stick	Round
Attribute 3 = Texture	Hard	Hard	Soft	Soft and juicy
Attribute 4 = Size	10 cm in length	3 cm radius	10 cm in length	3 cm radius
Attribute 5 = Taste	Sweet	Sweet	Bland	Sweet and sour

We just got introduced to supervised learning. We will relate this activity to the key steps of machine learning:

- **Define the ML problem**: Purchasing the correct classes of vegetables from all the classes of vegetables present in the store, based on the training and experience already gained on different attributes of the vegetables.
- **Prepare/gather the data and train the model**: The 15-year-old son has already been trained with sufficient knowledge of all the vegetables. This knowledge of all the different types of vegetables he has seen and eaten, and of their attributes and features, forms the historical training data for the problem, for the model—the 15-year-old son.

- **Evaluate the model**: The son is asked to purchase a few vegetables from the store. This is the test set provided to him to evaluate the model. The task of the model now is to identify the correct class label of the vegetables from the store based on the list provided.

There may be errors in the identification and purchase of correct vegetables in some cases. For example, the son might purchase double beans (a variant of beans) instead of ordinary beans. This may be due to a lack of sufficient training given to him on the distinguishing features between the beans and the double beans. If there is such an error, the parent would retrain him with the new type of vegetable, so that next time, he won't make that mistake.

So, we saw the basic concepts and functions of the supervised machine learning problem. Let's now get into the details of supervised learning.

Deep dive into supervised learning algorithms

Assume there are predictor attributes, *x1, x2, ... xn*, and also an objective attribute, y, for a given dataset. Then, the supervised learning is the machine learning task of finding the prediction function that takes as input both the predictor attributes and the objective attribute from this dataset, and is capable of mapping the predictive attributes to the objective attribute for even unseen data currently not in the training dataset with minimal error.

The data in the dataset used for arriving at the prediction function is called the **training data** and it consists of a set of training examples where each example consists of an input object, x (typically a vector), and a desired output value, y. A supervised learning algorithm analyzes the training data and produces an inferred function that maps the input to output and could also be used for mapping new, unseen example data:

$$Y = f(X) + error$$

The whole category of algorithms is called **supervised learning**, because here we consider both input and output variables for learning. So learning is supervised algorithm is by providing the input as well as the expected output in the training data for all the instances of training data.

The supervised algorithms have both predictor attributes and an objective function. The predictor attributes in a set of data items are those items that are considered to predict the objective function. The objective function is the goal of machine learning. This usually takes in the predictor attributes, perhaps with some other compute functionality, and would usually output a single numeric value.

Once we have defined a proper machine learning problem that would require supervised learning, the next step is to choose the machine learning algorithm that would solve the problem. This is the toughest task, because there is a huge list of learning algorithms present, and selecting the most suitable from among them is a nightmare.

Professor Pedro Domingos has provided a simple reference architecture (https://homes.cs.washington.edu/~pedrod/papers/cacm12.pdf), on which basis we could perform the algorithm selection using on three critical components that would be required for any machine learning algorithm, as follows:

- **Representation**: The way the model is represented so that it can be understood by the computer. It can also be considered as the hypothesis space within which the model would act.
- **Evaluation**: For each algorithm or model, there needs to be an evaluation or scoring function to determine which one performs better. The scoring function would be different for each type of algorithm.
- **Optimization**: A method to search among the models in the language for the highest-scoring one. The choice of optimization technique is integral to the efficiency of the learner, and also helps determine the model produced if the evaluation function has more than one optimum.

Supervised learning problems can be further grouped into regression and classification problems:

- **Classification**: When the output variable is a category, such as green or red, or good or bad.
- **Regression**: When the output variable is a real value, such as dollars or weight.

In this section, we will go through the following supervised learning algorithms with easy-to-understand examples:

- Naive Bayes
- Decision trees
- Linear regression

- Logistic regression
- Support vector machines
- Random forest

Naive Bayes

Naive Bayes is a powerful classification algorithm, implemented on the principles of Bayes theorem. It assumes that there is non-dependence between the feature variables considered in the dataset.

Bayes theorem describes the probability of an event, based on prior knowledge of conditions that might be related to the event. For example, if cancer is related to age, then, using Bayes theorem, a person's age can be used to more accurately assess the probability that they have cancer, compared to the assessment of the probability of cancer made without knowledge of the person's age.

A Naive Bayes classifier assumes that the presence of a particular feature in a class is unrelated to the presence of any other feature. For example, a vegetable may be considered to be a carrot if it is orange, cone-shaped, and about three inches in length. The algorithm is naive as it considers all of these properties independently to contribute to the probability that this vegetable is a carrot. Generally, features are not independent, but Naive Bayes considers them so for prediction.

Let's see a practical usage where the Naive Bayes algorithm is used. Let's assume we have several news feeds and we want to classify these feeds into cultural events and non-cultural. Let's consider the following sentences:

- *Dramatic event went well—cultural event*
- *This good public rally had a huge crowd—non-cultural event*
- *Music show was good—cultural event*
- *Dramatic event had a huge crowd—cultural event*
- *The political debate was very informative—non-cultural event*

When we are using Bayes theorem, all we want to do is use probabilities to calculate whether the sentences fall under cultural or non-cultural events.

As in the case of the carrot, we had features of color, shape, and size, and we treated all of them as independent to determine whether the vegetable considered is a carrot.

Similarly, to determine whether a feed is related to a cultural event, we take a sentence and then, from the sentence, consider each word as an independent feature.

Bayes' theorem states that $p(A|B) = p(B|A) \cdot P(A)/P(B)$, where *P(Cultural Event | Dramatic show good) = P(Dramatic show good | Cultural Event).P(Cultural event)/P(Dramatic show good)*.

We can discard the denominator here, as we are determining which tag has a higher probability in both cultural and non-cultural categories. The denominator for both cultural and non-cultural events is going to be the entire dataset and, hence, the same.

P(Dramatic show good) cannot be found, as this sentence doesn't occur in training data. So this is where the naive Bayes theorem really helps:

$$P(\text{Dramatic show good}) = P(\text{Dramatic}).P(\text{show}).P(\text{good})$$

$$P(\text{Dramatic show good/Cultural event}) = P(\text{Dramatic} | \text{cultural event}).P(\text{Show} | \text{cultural event}) | P(\text{good} | \text{cultural event})$$

Now it is easy to calculate these and determine the probability of whether the new news feed will be a cultural news feed or a political news feed:

$$P(\text{Cultural event}) = 3/5 \ (3 \text{ out of total 5 sentences})$$

$$P(\text{Non-cultural event}) = 2/5$$

$$P(\text{Dramatic/cultural event}) = \text{Counting how many times Dramatic appears in cultural event tags} = 2/13 \ (2 \text{ times dramatic appears in the total number of words of cultural event tags})$$

$$P(\text{Show/cultural event}) = 1/13$$

$$P(\text{good/cultural event}) = 1/13$$

There are various techniques, such as removing stop words, lemmatizing, n-grams, and TF-IDF, that can be used to make the feature identification of text classification more effective. We will be going through a few of them in the upcoming chapters.

Here is the final calculated summary:

Word	P(word l cultural event)	P(word l non-cultural event)
Dramatic	2/13	0
Show	1/13	0
Good	1/13	1/13

Now, we just multiply the probabilities and see which is bigger, and then fit the sentence into that category of tags.

So we know from the table that the tag is going to belong to the cultural event category, as that is what is going to result in a bigger product when the individual probabilities are multiplied.

These examples have given us a good introduction to the Naive Bayes theorem, which can be applied to the following areas:

- Text classification
- Spam filtering
- Document categorization
- Sentiment analysis in social media
- Classification of news articles based on genre

Decision trees

Decision tree algorithms are used for making decisions based on certain conditions. A decision tree is drawn upside down with its root at the top.

Let's take an organization's data where the feature set consists of certain software products along with their attributes—the time taken to build the product T, the effort taken to build the product E, and the cost taken to build the product C. It needs to be decided whether those products are to be built in the company or should be bought as products directly from outside the company.

Now, let's see how the decision tree could be created for this. In the following diagram, the bold text in black represents a condition/internal node, based on which the tree splits into branches/edges. The end of the branch that doesn't split any more is the decision/leaf.

Decision trees are used in program management, project management, and risk planning. Let's see a practical example. The following diagram shows the decision tree used by an organization for deciding which of its software needs to be built in-house or be purchased as products directly from outside. There are various decision points that need to be considered before making a decision and this can be represented in the form of a tree. The three features, cost, effort, and the schedule parameters, are considered to arrive at the decision as to **Buy** or **Build**:

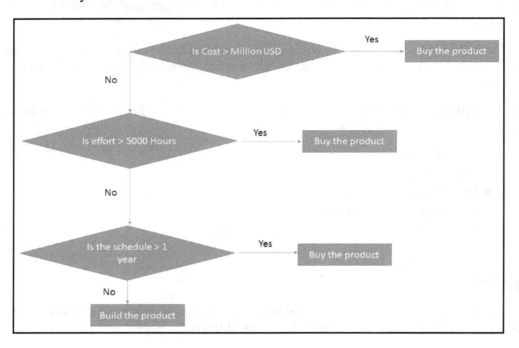

The preceding tree is called a **classification tree** as the aim is to classify a product nature as to buy or to build. **Regression trees** are represented in the same manner, only they predict continuous values, such as the price of a house. In general, decision tree algorithms are referred to as **CART** or **Classification and Regression Trees**.

Decision trees can be applied to the following areas:

- Risk identification
- Loan processing
- Election result prediction
- Process optimization
- Optional Pricing

Linear regression

Regression analysis linear regression is a statistical analysis method that finds relationships between variables. It helps us to understand the relationship between input and output numerical variables.

In this method, it is important to determine the dependent variables. For example, the value of the house (dependent variable) varies based on the size of the house; that is, how many square feet its area is (independent variable). The value of the house varies based on its location. Linear regression techniques can be useful for prediction.

Linear regression is used when the response is a continuous variable. The following diagram clearly shows how the linear regression for one variable work. The price of the house varies according to its size and is depicted in the following diagram:

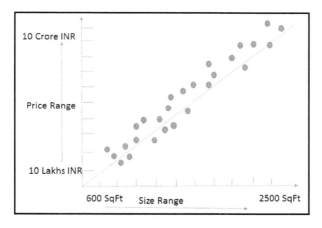

Linear regression can be applied to the following areas:

- Marketing
- Pricing
- Promotions
- Analyzing consumer behavior

Logistic regression

Logistic regression is a classification algorithm that is best suited to when the output to be predicted is a binary type—true or false, male or female, win or loss, and so on. Binary type means only two outcomes are possible.

The logistic regression is so called because of the sigmoid function used by the algorithm.

A logistic function or logistic curve is a common S shape (sigmoid curve), depicted by the following equation:

$$f(x) = \frac{L}{1 + e^{-k(x-x_0)}}$$

In the preceding equation, the symbols have the following meanings:

- e: The natural logarithm base (also known as **Euler's number**)
- x_0: The x-value of the sigmoid's midpoint
- L: The curve's maximum value
- k: The steepness of the curve

The standard logistic function is called a **sigmoid function**:

$$S(x) = \frac{1}{1 + e^{-x}}$$

The sigmoid curve is depicted here. It's an S-shaped curve:

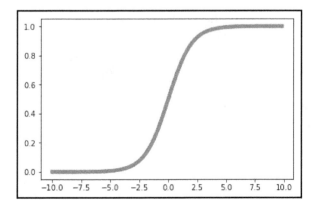

This curve has a finite limit of the following:

- *0* as *x* approaches −∞
- *1* as *x* approaches +∞

The output of the sigmoid function when *x=0* is *0.5*.

Thus, if the output is more than *0.5*, we can classify the outcome as 1 (or **YES**), and, if it is less than *0.5*, we can classify it as 0 (or **NO**). For example: if the output is *0.65*, in probability terms, it can be interpreted as—*There is a 65 percent chance that it is going to rain today.*

Thus, the output of the sigmoid function cannot just be used to classify yes/no; it can also be used to determine the probability of yes/no. It can be applied to the following areas:

- Image segmentation and categorization
- Geographic image processing
- Handwriting recognition
- Healthcare, for disease prediction and gene analytics
- Prediction in various areas where a binary outcome is expected

Support vector machines

A **support vector machine** (**SVM**) is a supervised machine learning algorithm that can be used for both classification and regression. SVMs are more commonly used for classification.

Given some data points, each belonging to one of the two binary classes, the goal is to decide which class a new data point will be in. We need to visualize the data point as a p-dimensional vector, and we need to determine whether we can separate two such data points with a (p-1) dimensional hyperplane.

There may be many hyper planes that separate such data points, and this algorithm will help us to arrive at the best hyperplane that provides the largest separation. This hyperplane is called the **maximum-margin hyperplane**, and the classifier is called the **maximum-margin classifier**. We can extend the concept of a separating hyperplane to develop a hyperplane that almost separates the classes, using a so-called **soft margin**. The generalization of the maximal margin classifier to the non-separable case is known as the **support vector classifier**.

Let's take the first example. In this, there is one hyperplane that separates the red dots and the blue dots:

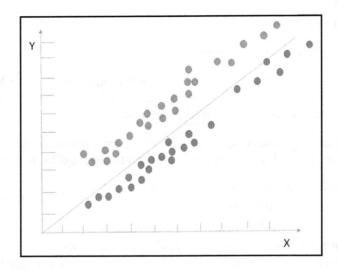

But imagine that the points were distributed as follows—how will we identify the hyperplane that separates the red dots and the blue dots:

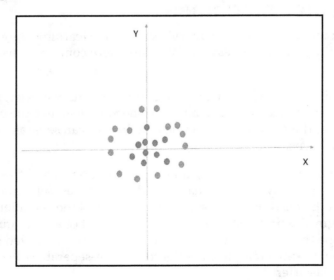

The solution is to identify the hyperplane with SVM. It can execute transformations to identify the hyperplane that separates the two for classification. It will introduce a new feature, z, which is $z=x^2+y^2$. Let's plot the graph with the x and z axes, and identify the hyperplane for classification:

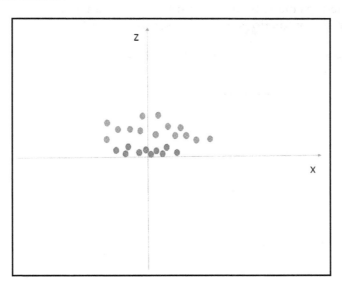

Now that we understand the basics of SVM, let's look at the areas where it can be applied:

- Face detection
- Image classification
- Bioinformatics
- Geological and environmental sciences
- Genetics
- Protein studies
- Handwriting recognition

Random forest

We have already seen what a decision tree is. Having understood decision trees, let's take a look at random forests. A random forest combines many decision trees into a single model. Individually, predictions made by decision trees (or humans) may not be accurate, but combined together, the predictions will be closer to the mark, on average.

The following diagram shows us a random forest, where there are multiple trees and each is making a prediction:

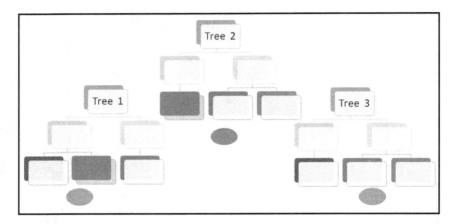

Random forest is a combination of many decision trees and, hence, there is a greater probability of having many views from all trees in the forest to arrive at the final desired outcome/prediction. If only a single decision tree is taken into consideration for prediction, there is less information considered for prediction. But in random forest, when there are many trees involved, the source of information is diverse and extensive. Unlike decision trees, random forests are not biased, since they are not dependent on one source.

The following diagram demonstrates the concept of random forests:

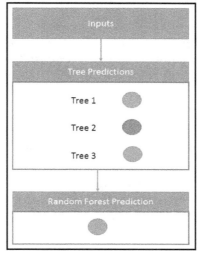

Random forests can be applied to the following areas:

- Risk identification
- Loan processing
- Election result prediction
- Process optimization
- Optional pricing

Introduction to unsupervised learning algorithms

Consider a scenario where a child is given a bag full of beads of different sizes, colors, shapes, and made of various materials. We just leave to the child do whatever they want with the whole bag of beads.

There are various things the child could do, based on their interests:

- Separate the beads into categories based on size
- Separate the beads into categories based on shape

- Separate the beads into categories based on a combination of color and shape
- Separate the beads into categories based on a combination of material, color, and shape

The possibilities are endless. However, the child without any prior teaching is able to go through the beads and uncover patterns of which it doesn't need any any prior knowledge at all. They are discovering the patterns purely on the basis of going through the beads at hand, that is, the data at hand. We just got introduced to unsupervised machine learning!

We will relate the preceding activity to the key steps of machine learning:

1. **Define the ML problem**: Uncover hidden patterns of beads from the given bag of beads.
2. **Prepare/gather the data and train the model**: The child opens the bagful of beads and understands what the bag contains. They discover the attributes of the different beads present:
    - Color
    - Shape
    - Size
    - Material
3. **Evaluate the model**: If a new set of beads is given to the child, how will they cluster these beads based on their previous experience of clustering beads?

There may be errors in grouping the beads that need to be corrected/fixed so that they don't recur in future.

So, now that we have seen the basic concepts and functions of the unsupervised machine learning problem, let's get into the details of unsupervised learning.

Deep dive into unsupervised learning algorithms

Unsupervised machine learning deals with learning unlabeled data—that is, data that has not been classified or categorized, and arriving at conclusions/patterns in relation to them.

These categories learn from test data that has not been labeled, classified, or categorized. Instead of responding to feedback, unsupervised learning identifies commonalities in the data and reacts based on the presence or absence of such commonalities in each new piece of data.

The input given to the learning algorithm is unlabeled and, hence, there is no straightforward way to evaluate the accuracy of the structure that is produced as output by the algorithm. This is one feature that distinguishes unsupervised learning from supervised learning.

> The unsupervised algorithms have predictor attributes but **NO** objective function.

What does it mean to learn without an objective? Consider the following:

- Explore the data for natural groupings.
- Learn association rules, and later examine whether they can be of any use.

Here are some classic examples:

- Performing market basket analysis and then optimizing shelf allocation and placement
- Cascaded or correlated mechanical faults
- Demographic grouping beyond known classes
- Planning product bundling offers

In this section, we will go through the following unsupervised learning algorithms with easy-to-understand examples:

- Clustering algorithms
- Association rule mapping

> **Principal component analysis** (**PCA**) and **singular value decomposition** (**SVD**) may also be of interest if you want to deep dive into those concepts.

Clustering algorithms

Clustering the dataset into useful groups is what clustering algorithms do. The goal of clustering is to create groups of data points, such that points in different clusters are dissimilar, while points within a cluster are similar.

There are two essential elements for clustering algorithms to work:

- **Similarity function**: This determines how we decide that two points are similar.
- **Clustering method**: This is the method observed in order to arrive at clusters.

There needs to be a mechanism to determine similarity between points, on which basis they could be categorized as similar or dissimilar. There are various similarity measures. Here are a few:

- **Euclidean**:

$$sim_{euclid}(\vec{d}_i, \vec{d}_j) = \left[\sqrt{\sum_{k=1,n} (d_{i,k}^2 - d_{j,k}^2)} \right]^{-1}$$

- **Cosine**:

$$sim_{cos}(\vec{q}, \vec{d}_i) = \frac{\vec{q} \bullet \vec{d}_i}{|\vec{q}|_2 \times |\vec{d}_i|_2}$$

- **KL-divergence**:

$$D(\vec{p}\|\vec{q}) \stackrel{def}{=} \sum_i p_i \log \frac{p_i}{q_i} = \sum_i p_i \log p_i - \sum_i p_i \log q_i$$
$$= -H(\vec{p}) + H(\vec{p}, \vec{q})$$

Clustering methods

Once we know the similarity measure, we next need to choose the clustering method. We will go through two clustering methods:

- Hierarchical agglomerative clustering methods
- K-means clustering

Hierarchical agglomerative clustering methods

Agglomerative hierarchical clustering is a classical clustering algorithm from the statistics domain. It involves iterative merging of the two most similar groups, which, in the first instance, contain single elements. The name of the algorithm refers to its way of working, as it creates hierarchical results in an agglomerative or bottom-up way, that is, by merging smaller groups into larger ones.

Here is the high-level algorithm for this method of clustering used in document clustering.

1. Generic agglomerative process (Salton, G: *Automatic Text Processing: The Transformation, Analysis, and Retrieval of Information by Computer*, Addison-Wesley, 1989) result in nested clusters via iterations.
2. Compute all pairwise document-document similarity coefficients
3. Place each of the n documents into a class of its own
4. Merge the two most similar clusters into one:
    - Replace the two clusters with the new cluster
    - Recompute inter-cluster similarity scores with regard to the new cluster
    - If the cluster radius is greater than maxsize, block further merging
5. Repeat the preceding step until there are only k clusters left (note: k could equal 1)

K-means clustering

The goal of this K-means clustering algorithm is to find K groups in the data, with each group having similar data points. The algorithm works iteratively to assign each data point to one of K groups based on the features that are provided. Data points are clustered based on feature similarity.

The K value is assigned randomly at the beginning of the algorithm and different variations of results could be obtained by altering the K value. Once the algorithm sequence of activities is initiated after the selection of K, as depicted in the following points, we find that there are two major steps that keep repeating, until there is no further scope for changes in the clusters.

The two major steps that get repeated are *Step 2* and *Step 3*, depicted as follows:

- **Step 2**: Assigning the data point from the dataset to any of the K clusters. This is done by calculating the distance of the data point from the cluster centroid. As specified, any one of the distance functions that we discussed already could be used for this calculation.
- **Step 3**: Here again, recalibration of the centroid occurs. This is done by taking the mean of all data points assigned to that centroid cluster.

The final output of the algorithm is K clusters that have similar data points:

1. Select *k-seeds $d(k_i, kj) > d_{min}$*

2. Assign points to clusters according to minimum distance:

$$Cluster(p_i) = Argmin(d(p_i, s_j))$$
$$s_j \epsilon s_1, \ldots, s_k$$

3. Compute new cluster centroids:

$$\overrightarrow{c_j} = \frac{1}{n} \sum_{p_i \epsilon j^{th} cluster}$$

4. Reassign points to the cluster (as in *Step 2*)
5. Iterate until no points change the cluster.

Here are some areas where clustering algorithms are used:

- City planning
- Earthquake studies
- Insurance
- Marketing
- Medicine, for the analysis of antimicrobial activity and medical imaging
- Crime analysis
- Robotics, for anomaly detection and natural language processing

Association rule learning algorithm

Association rule mining is more useful for categorical non-numeric data. Association rule mining is primarily focused on finding frequent co-occurring associations among a collection of items. It is sometimes also called **market-basket analysis**.

In a shopper's basket, the goal is to determine what items occur together frequently. This shows co-relations that are very hard to find from a random sampling method. The classic example of this is the famous Beer and Diapers association, which is often mentioned in data mining books. The scenario is this: men who go to the store to buy diapers will also tend to buy beer. This scenario is very hard to intuit or determine through random sampling.

Another example was discovered by Walmart in 2004, when a series of hurricanes crossed Florida. Walmart wanted to know what shoppers usually buy before a hurricane strikes. They found one particular item that increased in sales by a factor of seven over normal shopping days; that item was not bottled water, batteries, beer, flashlights, generators, or any of the usual things that we might imagine. The item was **strawberry pop tarts**! It is possible to conceive a multitude of reasons as to why this was the most desired product prior to the arrival of a hurricane–pop tarts do not require refrigeration, they do not need to be cooked, they come in individually wrapped portions, they have a long shelf life, they are a snack food, they are a breakfast food, kids love them, we love them, the list goes on. Despite these obvious reasons, it was still a huge surprise!

When mining for associations, the following could be useful:

- Search for rare and unusual co-occurring associations of non-numeric items.
- If the data is time-based data, consider the effects of introducing a time lag in data mining experiments to see whether the strength of the correlation reaches its peak at a later time.

Market-basket analysis can be applied to the following areas:

- Retail management
- Store management
- Inventory management
- NASA and environmental studies
- Medical diagnoses

Summary

In this chapter, we learned about what supervised learning is through a naive example and deep dived into concepts of supervised learning. We went through various supervised learning algorithms with practical examples and their application areas and then we started going through unsupervised learning with naive examples. We also covered the concepts of unsupervised learning and then we went through various unsupervised learning algorithms with practical examples and their application areas.

In the subsequent chapters, we will be solving mobile machine learning problems by using some of the supervised and unsupervised machine learning algorithms that we have gone through in this chapter. We will also be exposing you to mobile machine learning SDKs, which will be used to implement mobile machine learning solutions.

References

- Dr. Pedro Domingo's paper—https://homes.cs.washington.edu/~pedrod/papers/cacm12.pdf, summarizes twelve key lessons that machine learning researchers and practitioners have learned, including pitfalls to avoid, important issues to focus on, and answers to common questions in this area.

Random Forest on iOS

3

This chapter will provide you with an overview of the random forest algorithm. We will first look at the decision tree algorithm and, once we have a handle on it, try to understand the random forest algorithm. Then, we will use Core ML to create a machine learning program that leverages the random forest algorithm and predicts the possibility of a patient being diagnosed with breast cancer based on a given set of breast cancer patient data.

As we already saw in Chapter 1, *Introduction to Machine Learning on Mobile,* any machine learning program has four phases: define the machine learning problem, prepare the data, build/rebuild/test the model, and deploy it for usage. In this chapter, we will try to relate these with random forest and solve the underlying machine learning problem.

Problem definition: The breast cancer data for certain patients is provided and we want to predict the possibility of diagnosing breast cancer for a new data item.

We will be covering the following topics:

- Understanding decision trees and how to apply them to solve an ML problem
- Understanding decision trees through a sample dataset and Excel
- Understanding random forests
- Solving the problem using a random forest in Core ML:
    - Technical requirements
    - Creating a model file using the scikit-learn and pandas libraries
    - Testing the model
    - Importing the scikit-learn model into the Core ML project
    - Writing an iOS mobile application and using the scikit-learn model in it to perform the breast cancer prediction

Introduction to algorithms

In this section, we will look at the decision tree algorithm. We will go through an example to understand the algorithm. Once we get some clarity on the algorithm, we will try to understand the random forest algorithm with an example.

Decision tree

To understand the random forest model, we must first learn about the decision tree, the basic building block of a random forest. We all use decision trees in our daily lives, even if you don't know it by that name. You will be able to relate to the concepts of a decision tree once we start going through the example.

Imagine you approach a bank for a loan. The bank will scan you for a series of eligibility criteria before they approve the loan. For each individual, the loan amount they offer will vary, based on the different eligibility criteria they satisfy.

They may go ahead with various decision points to make the final decision to arrive at the possibility of granting a loan and the amount that can be given, such as the following:

- **Source of income**: Employed or self-employed?
- **If employed, place of employment**: Private sector or government sector?
- **If private sector, range of salary**: Low, medium, or high?
- **If government sector, range of salary**: Low, medium, or high?

There may be further questions, such as how long you've been employed with that company, or whether you have any outstanding loans. This process, in its most basic form, is a decision tree:

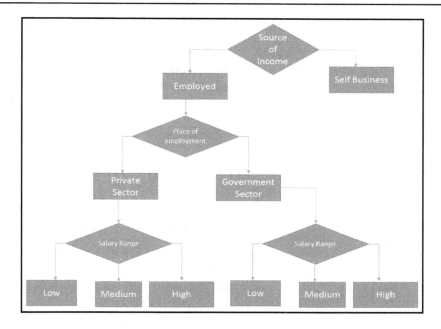

As you can see in the preceding diagram, a decision tree is a largely used non-parametric effective machine learning modeling technique for classification problems. To find solutions, a decision tree makes sequential, hierarchical decisions about the outcomes based on the predictor data.

For any given data item, a series of questions is asked, which leads to a class label or a value. This model asks a series of predefined questions of the incoming data item and, based on these answers, branches out to that series and proceeds until it arrives at the resulting data value or class label. The model is constructed based on the observed data, and there are no assumptions made about the distribution of the errors or the distribution of data itself.

In the decision tree models where the target variable uses a discrete set of values, this is called a **classification tree**. In these trees, each node, or leaf, represents class labels, while the branches represent features leading to class labels.

A decision tree where the target variable takes a continuous value, usually numbers, is called a **regression tree**.

These decision trees are well represented using **directed acyclic graphs** (**DAGs**). In these graphs, nodes represent decision points and edges are the connections between the nodes. In the preceding loan scenario, the salary range of $30,000-$70,000 would be an edge and the medium are nodes.

Advantages of the decision tree algorithm

The goal of the decision tree is to arrive at the optimal choice for the given problem. The final leaf node should be the best choice for the problem at hand. The algorithm behaves greedily and tries to come to the optimal choice in each decision it takes.

The whole problem is divided into multiple sub-problems, with each sub-problem branching out to other sub-problems. The subsets arrived are based on a parameter called **purity**. A node is said to be 100% pure when all decisions will lead to data belonging to the same class. It will be 100% impure when there is a possibility of splitting its subsets into categories. The goal of the algorithm is to reach 100% purity for each node in the tree.

The purity of a node is measured using Gini impurity, and Gini impurity is a standard metric that helps in splitting the node of a decision tree.

The other metric that would be used in a decision tree is information gain, which will be used to decide what feature of the dataset should be used to split at each step in the tree. The information gain is the decrease in entropy (randomness) after a dataset is split on an attribute. Constructing a decision tree is all about finding attributes that return the highest information gain, that is, the most homogeneous branches, which means all data belonging to the same subset or class.

Disadvantages of decision trees

The model stops only when all data points can fit into a single class/category. So there is a possibility that it may not generalize well for complex problems and the chance of bias is high.

These problems can be solved by defining the maximum depth of the tree or by specifying the minimum number of data points needed to split the node further in the tree.

Advantages of decision trees

The following are the advantages listed:

- Simple to understand and visualize
- Very easy to build and can handle both qualitative and quantitative data
- Easy to validate
- Computationally, it is not very expensive

 To summarize the decision tree model, we can conclude that it is basically a flowchart of questions leading to a prediction.

Random forests

Now, let's move from a single decision tree to a random forest. If you wanted to guess who the next President will be, how would you go about predicting this? Let's see the different kinds of questions that we would ask to predict this:

- How many candidates are there? Who are they?
- Who is the current President?
- How are they performing?
- Which party do they belong to?
- Is there any current movement against that party?
- In how many states the political party has probability to win
- Were they the incumbent President?
- What are the major voting issues?

Many questions like this will come to our mind and we will attach different weights/importance to them.

Each person's prediction to the preceding questions may be different. There are too many factors to take into account, and the possibility are, each person's guess will be different. Every person comes to these questions with different backgrounds and knowledge levels, and may interpret the question differently.

So there is chance of having a high variance for the answers. If we take all the predictions given by different individuals separately and then average them out, it becomes a random forest.

A random forest combines many decision trees into a single model. Individually, predictions made by decision trees (or humans) may not be accurate, but, when combined, the predictions will be closer to the mark, on average.

The following diagram will help us understand the voting prediction using the random forest algorithm:

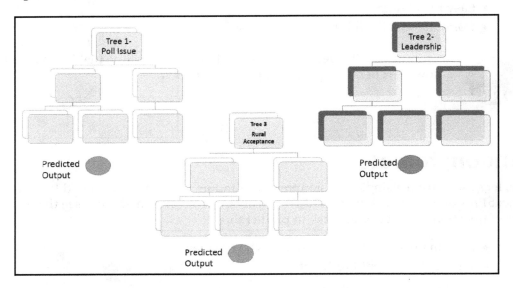

The following diagram gives a flowchart view of the previous diagram:

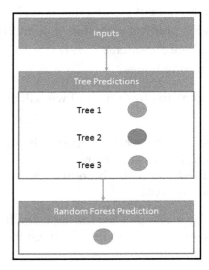

Let's look at why a random forest is better than a decision tree:

- A random forest is a combination of many decision trees and, hence, there is a greater probability that there would be many viewpoints to arrive at the final prediction.
- If only a single decision tree is considered for prediction, there is less information considered for prediction. But, in a random forest, when there are many trees involved, there is more information and it is more diverse.
- The random forest may not be biased, as may be the case with the decision tree, since it is not dependent on a single source.

Why the name random forest? Well, as much as people might rely on different sources to make a prediction, each decision tree in the forest considers a random subset of features when forming questions and only has access to a random set of the training data points. This increases diversity in the forest, leading to more robust overall predictions and hence, the name random forest.

Solving the problem using random forest in Core ML

In this section, we will try to understand the random forest through a detailed example with a specific dataset. We are going to use the same dataset to work out the iOS Core ML example.

Dataset

We will use the breast cancer dataset for the random forest problem. Features are computed from a digitized image of a **fine needle aspirate** (**FNA**) of a breast mass. They describe the characteristics of the cell nuclei present in the image. The dataset can be found at `https://archive.ics.uci.edu/ml/datasets/Breast+Cancer+Wisconsin+(Diagnostic)`.

Naming the dataset

We will be using the Breast Cancer dataset. The following list contains the various conventions used in the dataset:

- ID number
- Diagnosis (*M* = malignant, and *B* = benign)

- 10 real-valued features are computed for each cell nucleus:
  - Radius (mean of the distances from the center to points on the perimeter)
  - Texture (standard deviation of gray scale values)
  - Perimeter
  - Area
  - Smoothness (local variation in radius lengths)
  - Compactness (*perimeter^2/area - 1.0*)
  - Concavity (severity of concave portions of the contour)
  - Concave points (number of concave portions of the contour)
  - Symmetry
  - Fractal dimension (coastline approximation-1)

We will use random forest through Excel, applying the breast cancer dataset, to understand random forest in detail. We will consider only data elements from 569 sample pieces of data from the breast cancer dataset for the purposes of analysis.

Technical requirements

The following software needs to be installed on the developer machine:

- Python
- Xcode in the macOS environment

The exercise programs for the chapter can be found on the GitHub repository (`https://github.com/PacktPublishing/Machine-Learning-for-Mobile`) under the `Chapter03` folder. Let's start by entering the command to install the Python package:

```
pip install pandas
pip install -U scikit-learn
pip install -U pandas
```

Then, issue the command to install `coremltools`:

```
pip install -U coremltools
```

Creating the model file using scikit-learn

This section will explain how we are going to create the random forest model file using scikit-learn and convert it into the `.mlmodel` file that is compatible with Core ML. We are going to use the Breast Cancer dataset to create the model. The following is a Python program that creates a simple random forest model using scikit-learn and the Breast Cancer dataset. Then, the Core ML tools convert it into the Core ML—compatible model file. Let's go through the program in detail.

First, we need to import the required packages:

```
# importing required packages
import numpy as np
```

NumPy is the fundamental package for scientific computing with Python. It contains a powerful N-dimensional array object. This `numpy` array will be used in this program for storing the dataset, which has 14 dimensions:

```
import pandas as pd
from pandas.core import series
```

Here, we are using pandas (`https://pandas.pydata.org/pandas-docs/stable/10min.html`) which is an open source, BSD-licensed library providing high-performing, easy-to-use data structures and data analysis tools for the Python programming language. Using pandas, we can create a data frame. You can assume that a pandas dataframe is an Excel sheet in which every sheet has headings and data.

Now, let's move on to understand the program written for solving the machine learning problem at hand:

```
from sklearn.ensemble import RandomForestClassifier

from sklearn.metrics import accuracy_score
import sklearn.datasets as dsimport sklearn.datasets as ds
```

The preceding lines import the `sklearn` packages. Now, we will import built-in datasets in the `sklearn` package:

```
dataset = ds.load_breast_cancer()
```

The preceding line loads the Breast Cancer dataset from the `sklearn` dataset package:

```
cancerdata = pd.DataFrame(dataset.data)
```

This will create a dataframe from the data present in the dataset. Let's assume that the dataset is an Excel sheet with rows and columns with column headings:

```
cancerdata.columns = dataset.feature_names
```

The following piece of code will add the column headings to the columns in the dataset:

```
for i in range(0,len(dataset.feature_names)):
if ['mean concave points', 'mean area', 'mean radius', 'mean perimeter',
'mean concavity'].\
__contains__(dataset.feature_names[i]):
continue
else:
cancerdata = cancerdata.drop(dataset.feature_names[i], axis=1)
```

The preceding lines will delete all the columns other than the following:

- Mean concave points
- Mean area
- Mean radius
- Mean perimeter
- Mean concavity

To reduce the number of feature columns in the dataset, I am deleting some of the columns that have less impact on the model:

```
cancerdata.to_csv("myfile.csv")
```

This line will save the data to a CSV file; you can open it and see in Excel to find out what is present in the dataset:

```
cancer_types = dataset.target_names
```

In the Excel dataset, when you examine it, you will know that the diagnosis will include the value as 0 or 1, where 0 is malignant and 1 is benign. To change these numeric values to the real names, we write the following piece of code:

```
cancer_names = []
//getting all the corresponding cancer types with name [string] format.
for i in range(len(dataset.target)):
cancer_names.append(cancer_types[dataset.target[i]])
x_train, x_test, y_train, y_test =
sklearn.model_selection.train_test_split(cancerdata,cancer_names,test_size=
0.3, random_state=5)
```

This line of code will split the dataset into two—one for training and one for testing, and will save it in the corresponding variables defined for the purpose:

```
classifier = RandomForestClassifier()
```

The following will create a classifier:

```
classifier.fit(x_train, y_train)
```

This code will feed the training data and train the model:

```
//testing the model with test data
print(classifier.predict(x_test))
```

The preceding line will print the predicted cancer types for the testing data to the console, as shown here:

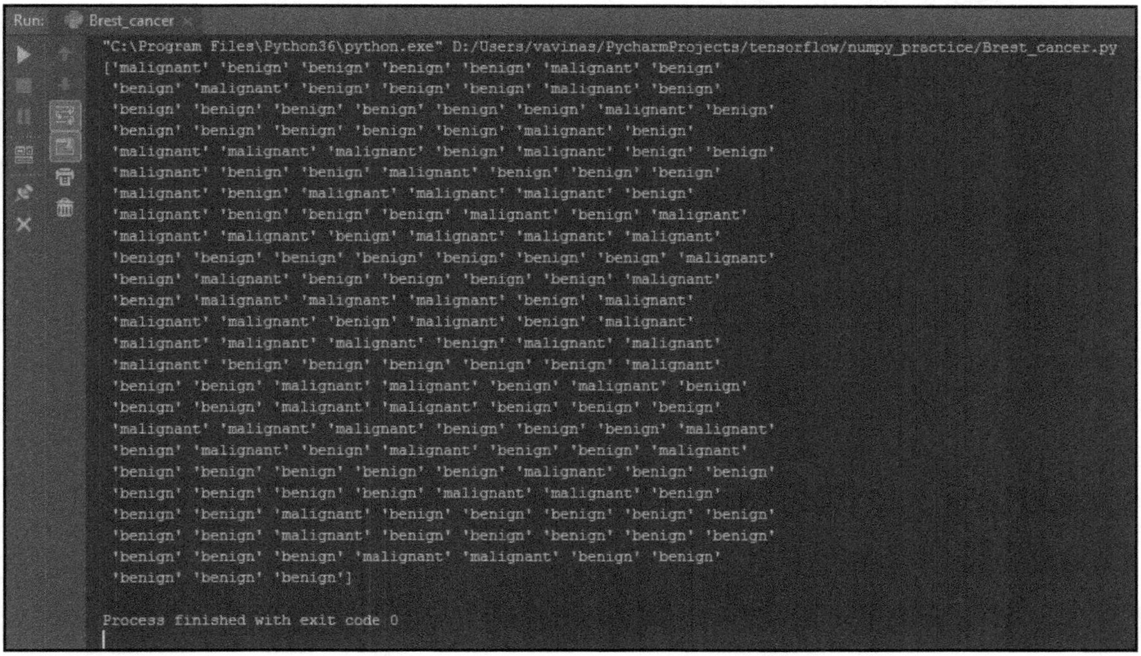

Converting the scikit model to the Core ML model

Let me explain using an example: let's assume you're from France and you only speak French and English. Imagine you went to India on vacation. And you went to your hotel restaurant, where the waiter offered you a menu that was written in a local language. Now, what would you do? Let me guess, you'd ask the waiter, or another customer/your tour guide, to explain the items to you, or you simply scan the images in Google translate.

My point is that you need a translator. That's it. Similarly, in order for the scikit model to be understood by the iOS mobile application, a converter that will translate it to the Core ML format is required.

That's all the work of the following code. It will convert the scikit-learn format to the Core ML format:

```
//converting the fitted model to a Core ML Model file

model = coremltools.converters.sklearn.convert(classifier,
input_features=list(cancerdata.columns.values),
output_feature_names='typeofcancer')

model.save("cancermodel.mlmodel")
```

For this, to work, you have to install `coremltools` using your `pip`. Then, write the following code on the top to import it:

```
import coremltools
```

Once you run this program, you will get a model file in your disk, named `cancermodel.mlmodel`, which you'll use in your iOS project for inference.

Creating an iOS mobile application using the Core ML model

In this section, we will be creating an iOS project to use Core ML, for which you will require Xcode (it must be version 9+).

Let's get started by opening Xcode and creating an empty swift application with a storyboard. In the main storyboard design, the screen will appear as follows. Then, add the generated model file to your project. This should give you the following structure:

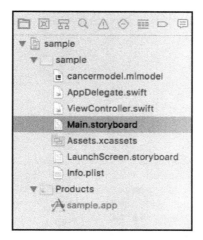

Now, create the UI in your main storyboard file, as shown here:

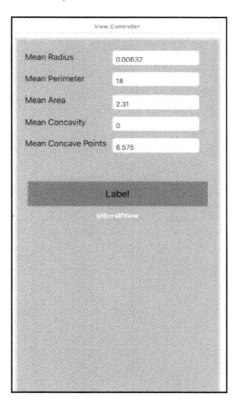

Create outlets for each text field. And add event listener to each and every text field. Now, your view controller will look like this:

```
import UIKit
import Core ML
class ViewController: UIViewController {
    let model = cancermodel()
    @IBOutlet weak var meanradius: UITextField!
    @IBOutlet weak var cancertype: UILabel!
    @IBOutlet weak var meanperimeter: UITextField!
    @IBOutlet weak var meanarea: UITextField!
    @IBOutlet weak var meanconcavity: UITextField!
    @IBOutlet weak var meanconcavepoints: UITextField!
    override func didReceiveMemoryWarning() {
        super.didReceiveMemoryWarning()
        // Dispose of any resources that can be recreated.
    }
    override func viewDidLoad() {
        super.viewDidLoad();
        updated(meanconcavepoints);
        //This line is to fire the initial update of the cancer type.
    }
    /*
This method will send the input data to your generated model class and
display the returned result to the label.
*/

    @IBAction func updated(_ sender: Any) {
        guard let modeloutput = try? model.prediction(mean_radius:
        Double(meanradius.text!)!, mean_perimeter:
        Double(meanperimeter.text!)!, mean_area: Double(meanarea.text!)!,
        mean_concavity: Double(meanconcavity.text!)!, mean_concave_points:
        Double(meanconcavepoints.text!)!) else {
            fatalError("unexpected runtime error")
        }
        cancertype.text = modeloutput.typeofcancer;
    }
}
```

You can find the same code in the GitHub repository for this book.

If you encounter any issue while building. Like signing or certificate, please google it or write to us.

Once you set up the project in Xcode, you can run it in the simulator. The result will look like this:

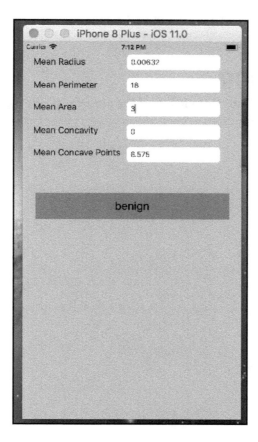

Summary

In this chapter, we learned about decision trees and random forests, and the differences between them. We also explored a decision tree through a sample dataset and Excel using a sample dataset and used random forest algorithm to it in order to establish the prediction. We used Core ML to write the iOS program, and then we applied the scikit-learn to create the model and converted the scikit model to the Core ML model using Core ML tools.

In the next chapter, we will learn more about TensorFlow and its use in Android.

Further reading

We can get further insight into Core ML and the services it offers by visiting their official website: `https://developer.apple.com/documentation/coreml`.

TensorFlow Mobile in Android 4

In the previous chapter, we focused on supervised learning and unsupervised learning, and learned about the different types of learning algorithms. In this chapter, we will get introduced to TensorFlow for mobile, and go through a sample program implementation using TensorFlow for mobile. In Chapter 9, *Neural Networks on Mobile*, we will be using it to implement a classification algorithm. But we need to understand how TensorFlow for mobile works and be able to write samples using it before we can implement machine learning algorithms with it. The objective of this chapter is to get introduced to TensorFlow, TensorFlow Lite, TensorFlow for mobile, and their ways of working, and to try hands-on examples using TensorFlow for mobile in Android.

In this chapter, we will cover the following topics:

- An introduction to TensorFlow, TensorFlow Lite, and TensorFlow for mobile
- The components of TensorFlow for mobile
- The architecture of a mobile machine learning application
- Building a sample program using TensorFlow for mobile in Android

By the end of this chapter, you will know how to build an application using TensorFlow for mobile in Android. We will walk through using it in order to implement a classification algorithm in Chapter 9, *Neural Networks on Mobile*.

An introduction to TensorFlow

TensorFlow is a tool to implement machine learning developed by Google, and was open sourced in 2015. It is a product that can be installed on desktops and can be used to create machine learning models. Once the model has been built and trained on the desktop, the developer can transfer these models to mobile devices and start using them to predict results in mobile applications by integrating them into iOS and Android mobile applications. There are currently two flavors of TensorFlow available for implementing machine learning solutions on mobile and embedded devices:

- **Mobile devices**: TensorFlow for Mobile
- **Mobile and Embedded devices**: TensorFlow Lite

The following table will help you to understand the key differences between TensorFlow for mobile and TensorFlow Lite:

TensorFlow for Mobile	TensorFlow Lite
Designed to work with larger devices.	Designed to work with really small devices.
Binary is optimized for mobile.	Binary is really very small in size optimized for mobile and embedded devices, minimal dependencies, and enhanced performance.
Enables deployment in CPU, GPU, and TPU across Android, iOS, and Raspberry Pi.	Supports hardware acceleration. Deployment possible on iOS, Android, and Raspberry Pi.
Recommended for usage now in mobile devices for production deployments.	Still under Beta and is undergoing improvements.
Wider operator and ML model support available.	Limited operators supported, and not all ML models are supported.

TensorFlow Lite components

In this section, we will go through the details of TensorFlow Lite: the overall architecture, the key components, and their functionality.

The following diagram provides a high-level overview of the key components and how they interact to bring machine learning to mobile devices:

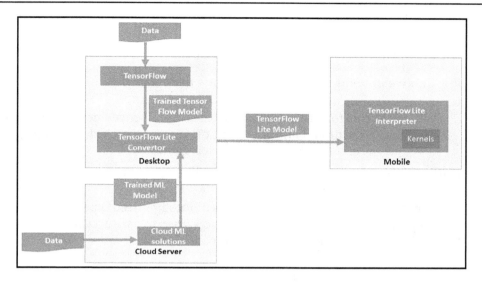

The following are the key steps to be followed when implementing ML on devices:

1. Use the TensorFlow, or any other machine learning framework, to create the trained TensorFlow/ML models on the desktop. The trained model can also be created using any Cloud ML engine.
2. Use the TensorFlow Lite converter to convert the trained ML model to the TensorFlow Lite model file.
3. Write a mobile application using these files and convert it into a package for deployment and execution in mobile devices. These lite files could be interpreted and executed directly in the kernels or in the hardware accelerators, if available in the device.

The following are the key components of TensorFlow Lite:

- Model-file format
- Interpreter
- Ops/kernel
- Interface to hardware acceleration

Model-file format

The following are the highlights of the model-file format:

- It is lightweight and has very few software dependencies.
- It supports quantization.
    - This format is FlatBuffer-based and, hence, increases the speed of execution. FlatBuffer is an open source project by Google, originally designed for video games.
- FlatBuffer is a cross-platform serialization library and is similar to protocol buffers.
- This format is more memory-efficient as it does not need a parsing/unpacking step to perform a secondary representation prior to data access. There is no marshaling step and, hence, it uses less code.

Interpreter

The following are the highlights of the interpreter:

- It is a mobile-optimized interpreter.
- It helps to keep mobile apps lean and fast.
- It uses a static-graph ordering and a custom (less dynamic) memory allocator to ensure minimal load, initialization, and execution latency.
- The interpreter has a static memory plan and a static execution plan.

Ops/Kernel

A set of core operators, both quantized and float, many of which have been tuned for mobile platforms. These can be used to create and run custom models. Developers can also write their own custom operators and use them in models.

Interface to hardware acceleration

TensorFlow Lite has an interface to hardware accelerators; in Android, it is through the Android Neural Network API and, in iOS, it is through CoreML.

The following are the pretested models that are guaranteed to work out of the box with TensorFlow Lite:

- **Inception V3**: A popular model for detecting the dominant objects present in an image.

- **MobileNets:** Computer vision models that can be used for classification, detection, and segmentation. MobileNet models are smaller, but less accurate, than Inception V3.

- **On-device smart reply**: An on-device model that provides one-touch replies for an incoming text message by suggesting contextually-relevant messages.

The architecture of a mobile machine learning application

Now that we understand the components of TensorFlow Lite, we'll look at how a mobile application works with the TensorFlow components to provide the mobile ML solution.

The mobile application should leverage the TensorFlow Lite model file to perform the inference for future data. The TensorFlow Lite model file can either be packaged with the mobile application and deployed together, or kept separate from the mobile application deployment package. The following diagram depicts the two possible deployment scenarios:

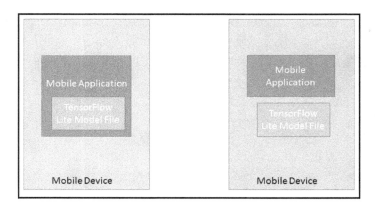

Each deployment has its pros and cons. In the first case, where both are coupled, there is more security for the model file and it can be kept safe and secured. This is a more straightforward approach. However, the application package size is increased due to the size of the model file. In the second case, where both are kept separate, it is easy to update the model file separately, without performing an application upgrade. Hence, all activities with respect to the application upgrade, deployment to the app store, and so on can be avoided for a model upgrade. The application package size can also be minimized due to this separation. However, since the model file is standalone, it should be handled with greater care, without leaving it vulnerable to security threats.

Having got an overview of the mobile application with the TensorFlow Lite model file, let's look at the whole picture. The mobile application is packaged with the TensorFlow Lite model file. This interaction between the mobile application written using the Android SDK and the TensorFlow Lite model file happens through the TensorFlow Lite Interpreter, which is part of the Android NDK layer. The C functions are invoked through the interfaces exposed to the SDK layer from the mobile application in order to do the prediction or inference by using the trained TensorFlow Lite model deployed with the mobile application. The following diagram provides a clear view of the layers of the SDK and NDK of the Android ecosystem that will be involved in a typical machine learning program. The execution can also be triggered on GPU or any specialized processors through the android NN layer:

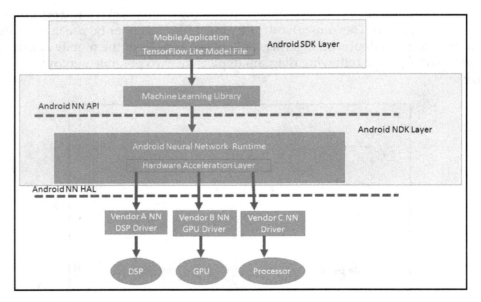

Understanding the model concepts

Before writing our first program using TensorFlow, we will briefly go through the concepts that will help us to understand how the TensorFlow Lite model work. We won't be going into the details, but a conceptual high level overview alone for better understanding.

MobileNet and Inception V3 are the built-in models that are based on **convolutional neural networks (CNNs)**.

At its most basic level, CNN can be thought of as a kind of neural network that uses many identical copies of the same neuron. This allows the network to have lots of neurons and express computationally large models while keeping the number of actual parameters – the values describing how neurons behave – that need to be learned fairly low.

This concept can be understood with the analogy of a Jigsaw puzzle and how we usually solve one. The following diagram is a puzzle that needs to be solved:

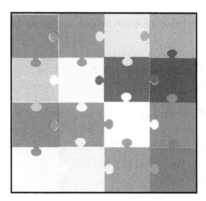

If we have to assemble this puzzle from the pieces provided, just think about how you will start solving it. You may group all the pieces with different colors together. Then within the same color, you'd check for patterns and then assemble them. This is the same way that convolutional networks train for image classification and recognition. Hence there is only a small portion, each neuron remembers. But the parent neuron understands how the things within its scope needs to be assembled to get the big picture.

In the Inception V3 and the MobileNet models, both work based on the CNN concept. The model is pretty much trained and stable. All we need to do to use our set of images is retrain the model with our images. So now that we have had enough of concepts and theory, we will move on to writing our first sample program using TensorFlow Lite for Android.

We will be using the TensorFlow for mobile for a classification application in Chapter 9, *Neural Networks on Mobile*

Writing the mobile application using the TensorFlow model

What we are going to do?

In this section, we are going to build a small $(a+b)2$ model in TensorFlow, deploy it into an android mobile application, and run it from the Android mobile device.

What do you need to know?

To proceed in this section, you need a working installation of Python, TensorFlow dependencies, and android studio, and also some knowledge of python and java android. You can find the instructions on how to install TensorFlow here: https://www.tensorflow.org/install/.

If you need a detailed installation procedure for Windows, please refer to the one provided with screenshots in the Chapter 11, *The Future of ML on Mobile Applications* of this book.

We saw the details of TensorFlow already. To put it onto a simple words TensorFlow is nothing but saving the tensor flow program written in python into a small file that can be read by the C++ native libraries what we will install in our Android app and can execute and do the inference from the mobile. To do so, JNI (Java native interface) is working as a bridge between java and C++.

To learn more about the idea behind tensor flow lite, check out https://www.tensorflow.org/mobile/tflite/.

Writing our first program

In order to write a TensorFlow mobile application, there are a few steps that we need to follow:

1. Create the TF (TensorFlow) model
2. Save the model
3. Freeze the graph

4. Optimize the model
5. Write the Android application and execute it

We will go through each of the steps in detail now.

Creating and Saving the TF model

First, we first create a simple model and save its computation graph as a serialized `GraphDef` file. After training the model, we then save the values of its variables into a checkpoint file. We have to turn these two files into an optimized standalone file, which is all we need to use inside the Android app.

For this tutorial, we create a very simple TensorFlow graph that implements a small use case that will calculate $(a+b)^2=c$. Here, we are saving the input as *a* and *b*, and the output as *c*.

To implement this sample program, we are going to use Python. So, as a prerequisite, you need to install python in your machine and install the TensorFlow libraries on your machine using `pip`.

Please check the software installations/appendix section of this book for instructions on how to install Python. `pip` is a python package manager that comes with Python.

Once you install python and set the path correctly, you can run the `pip` command from the command prompt. To install TensorFlow, run the following command:

```
pip install tensorflow
```

This sample might seem too simple and might not contain anything related to machine learning, but this example should be a good starting point to understand the concepts of TensorFlow and its working:

```
import tensorflow as tf
a = tf.placeholder(tf.int32, name='a') # input
b = tf.placeholder(tf.int32, name='b') # input
times = tf.Variable(name="times", dtype=tf.int32, initial_value=2)
c = tf.pow(tf.add(a, b), times, name="c")
saver = tf.train.Saver()

init_op = tf.global_variables_initializer() with tf.Session() as sess:
sess.run(init_op) tf.train.write_graph(sess.graph_def, '.',
'tfdroid.pbtxt')
```

```
sess.run(tf.assign(name="times", value=2, ref=times)) # save the graph
# save a checkpoint file, which will store the above assignment
saver.save(sess, './tfdroid.ckpt')
```

In the preceding program, we are creating two placeholders, named *a* and *b*, that can hold integer values. For now, just you can imagine placeholders as nodes in a tree for a decision tree. In the next line, we are creating a variable named times. We are creating this to store how many times we need to multiply the input. In this case, we are giving two as agenda is to do for $(a+b)^2$.

In the next line, we are applying addition operation on both the *a* and *b* nodes. And for that sum, we are applying power operation and saving the result in a new node called c. To run the code, first save it in a file with the .py extension. Then execute the program using the python command, as follows:

```
python (filename)
```

Running the previous piece of code will produce two files. First, it saves the TF computation graph in a GraphDef text file called tfdroid.pbtxt. Next, it will perform a simple assignment (which normally would be done through actual learning) and save a checkpoint of the model variables in tfdroid.ckpt.

Freezing the graph

Now that we have these files, we need to freeze the graph by converting the variables in the checkpoint file into Const Ops that contain the values of the variables, and combining them with the GraphDef in a standalone file. Using this file makes it easier to load the model inside a mobile app. TensorFlow provides freeze_graph in tensorflow.python.tools for this purpose:

```
import sys import tensorflow as tf from tensorflow.python.tools
import freeze_graph from tensorflow.python.tools
import optimize_for_inference_lib MODEL_NAME = 'tfdroid'
# Freeze the graph

input_graph_path = MODEL_NAME+'.pbtxt' checkpoint_path =
'./'+MODEL_NAME+'.ckpt' input_saver_def_path = "" input_binary = False
output_node_names = "c" restore_op_name = "save/restore_all"
filename_tensor_name = "save/Const:0" output_frozen_graph_name =
'frozen_'+MODEL_NAME+'.pb' output_optimized_graph_name =
'optimized_'+MODEL_NAME+'.pb' clear_devices = True
freeze_graph.freeze_graph(input_graph_path, input_saver_def_path,
input_binary, checkpoint_path, output_node_names, restore_op_name,
filename_tensor_name, output_frozen_graph_name, clear_devices, "")
```

Optimizing the model file

Once we have the frozen graph, we can further optimize the file for inference-only purposes by removing the parts of the graph that are only needed during training. According to the documentation, this includes:

- Removing training-only operations, such as checkpoint saving
- Stripping out parts of the graph that are never reached
- Removing debug operations, such as CheckNumerics
- Folding batch normalization ops into the pre-calculated weights
- Fusing common operations into unified versions

TensorFlow provides optimize_for_inference_lib in tensorflow.python.tools for this purpose:

```
# Optimize for inference
input_graph_def = tf.GraphDef() with
tf.gfile.Open(output_frozen_graph_name, "r") as f: data = f.read()
input_graph_def.ParseFromString(data)
output_graph_def = optimize_for_inference_lib.optimize_for_inference(
input_graph_def, ["a", "b"],
# an array of the input node(s) ["c"],
# an array of output nodes tf.int32.as_datatype_enum)

# Save the optimized graph f =
tf.gfile.FastGFile(output_optimized_graph_name, "w")
f.write(output_graph_def.SerializeToString())
tf.train.write_graph(output_graph_def, './', output_optimized_graph_name)
```

Take note of the input and output nodes in the preceding code. Our graph only has one input node, named I, and one output node, named O. These names correspond to the names you use when you define your tensors. You should adjust these based on your graph in case you are using a different one.

Now we have a binary file, called optimized_tfdroid.pb, which means we are ready to build our Android app. If you got an exception when creating optimized_tfdroid.pb, you can use tfdroid.somewhat, which is an unoptimized version of the model – it is fairly large.

Creating the Android app

We need to get the TensorFlow libraries for Android, create an Android app, configure it to use these libraries, and then invoke the TensorFlow model inside the app.

Although you can compile the TensorFlow libraries from scratch, it's easier to use the prebuilt libraries.

Now use Android Studio to create an Android project with an empty activity.

Once the project is created, add the TF Libraries to the project's `libs` folder. You can get these libraries from the GitHub repository: `https://github.com/PacktPublishing/Machine-Learning-for-Mobile/tree/master/tensorflow%20simple/TensorflowSample/app/libs`.

Now your project's `libs/` folder should look like this:

```
libs
|_____arm64-v8a
|  |____libtensorflow_inference.so
|_____armeabi-v7a
|  |____libtensorflow_inference.so
|_____libandroid_tensorflow_inference_java.jar
|_____x86
|  |____libtensorflow_inference.so
|_____x86_64
|  |____libtensorflow_inference.so
```

You need to let your build system know where these libraries are located by putting the following lines inside of the Android block in `app/build.gradle`:

```
sourceSets { main { jniLibs.srcDirs = ['libs'] } }
```

Copying the TF Model

Create an Android Asset Folder for the app and place the `optimized_tfdroid.pb` or `tfdroid.pb` file that we just created inside it (`app/src/main/assets/`).

Creating an activity

Click on the project and create an empty activity named `MainActivity`. In the layout of that activity, paste the following XML:

```xml
<?xml version="1.0" encoding="utf-8"?>
<RelativeLayout xmlns:android="http://schemas.android.com/apk/res/android"
xmlns:tools="http://schemas.android.com/tools"
android:id="@+id/activity_main"
android:layout_width="match_parent"
android:layout_height="match_parent"
android:paddingBottom="@dimen/activity_vertical_margin"
android:paddingLeft="@dimen/activity_horizontal_margin"
android:paddingRight="@dimen/activity_horizontal_margin"
android:paddingTop="@dimen/activity_vertical_margin"
tools:context="com.example.vavinash.tensorflowsample.MainActivity">

<EditText
android:id="@+id/editNum1"
android:layout_width="100dp"
android:layout_height="wrap_content"
android:layout_alignParentTop="true"
android:layout_marginEnd="13dp"
android:layout_marginTop="129dp"
android:layout_toStartOf="@+id/button"
android:ems="10"
android:hint="a"
android:inputType="textPersonName"
android:textAlignment="center" />

<EditText
android:id="@+id/editNum2"
android:layout_width="100dp"
android:layout_height="wrap_content"
android:layout_alignBaseline="@+id/editNum1"
android:layout_alignBottom="@+id/editNum1"
android:layout_toEndOf="@+id/button"
android:ems="10"
android:hint="b"
android:inputType="textPersonName"
android:textAlignment="center" />

<Button
android:text="Run"
android:layout_width="wrap_content"
android:layout_height="wrap_content"
android:id="@+id/button"
android:layout_below="@+id/editNum2"
```

```
android:layout_centerHorizontal="true"
android:layout_marginTop="50dp" />

<TextView
android:layout_width="wrap_content"
android:layout_height="wrap_content"
android:text="Output"
android:id="@+id/txtViewResult"
android:layout_marginTop="85dp"
android:textAlignment="center"
android:layout_alignTop="@+id/button"
android:layout_centerHorizontal="true" />
</RelativeLayout>
```

In the `mainactivity.java` file, paste the following code:

```java
package com.example.vavinash.tensorflowsample;
import android.support.v7.app.AppCompatActivity;
import android.os.Bundle;
import android.widget.EditText;
import android.widget.TextView;
import android.widget.Button;
import android.view.View;
import org.tensorflow.contrib.android.TensorFlowInferenceInterface;public
class MainActivity extends AppCompatActivity {
    //change with the file name of your own model generated in python
tensorflow.
    private static final String MODEL_FILE =
"file:///android_asset/tfdroid.pb";

    //here we are using this interface to perform the inference with our
generated model. It internally     uses c++ libraries and JNI.
    private TensorFlowInferenceInterface inferenceInterface;
    static {
        System.loadLibrary("tensorflow_inference");
    }
    @Override
    protected void onCreate(Bundle savedInstanceState) {
        super.onCreate(savedInstanceState);
        setContentView(R.layout.activity_main);
        inferenceInterface = new TensorFlowInferenceInterface();
        //instantiatind and setting our model file as input.
        inferenceInterface.initializeTensorFlow(getAssets(), MODEL_FILE);
        final Button button = (Button) findViewById(R.id.button);
        button.setOnClickListener(new View.OnClickListener() {
            public void onClick(View v) {
                final EditText editNum1 = (EditText)
findViewById(R.id.editNum1);
```

```
                    final EditText editNum2 = (EditText)
findViewById(R.id.editNum2);
                    float num1 =
Float.parseFloat(editNum1.getText().toString());
                    float num2 =
Float.parseFloat(editNum2.getText().toString());
                    int[] i = {1};
                    int[] a = {((int) num1)};
                    int[] b = {((int) num2)};
                    //Setting input for variable a and b in our model.
                    inferenceInterface.fillNodeInt("a",i,a);
                    inferenceInterface.fillNodeInt("b",i,b);
                    //performing the inference and getting the output in
variable c
                    inferenceInterface.runInference(new String[] {"c"});
                    //reading received output
                    int[] c = {0};
                    inferenceInterface.readNodeInt("c", c);
                    //projecting to user.
                    final TextView textViewR = (TextView)
findViewById(R.id.txtViewResult);
                    textViewR.setText(Integer.toString(c[0]));
                }
            });
        }
}
```

In the preceding program, we are loading the TensorFlow binaries using the following snippet:

```
System.loadLibrary("tensorflow_inference");
```

In the create Bundle method, we have the main logic. Here, we are creating the TensorFlow inference object by supplying the TensorFlow model's .pb file, which has been generated and we saw that in the section - create and save model

Then we registered a click event to the **Run** button. In this, we are feeding the values to the a and b nodes in TensorFlow and running the inference, then we fetch the value in the C node and show it to the user.

Now run the app to see the results of the $(a+b)2 = c$ expression:

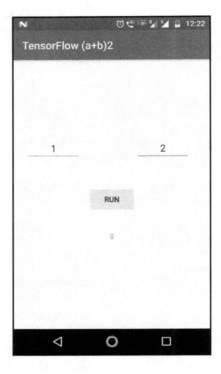

On the left side, it is showing the app's opening screen. In the provided text boxes, we need to give the a and b values. Once you click on the **Run** button, you will see the result in the output area.

You can get the preceding app code from the GitHub repository: `https://github.com/PacktPublishing/Machine-Learning-for-Mobile/tree/master/tensorflow%20simple`.

Summary

In this chapter, we got introduced to Google's machine learning tools for Mobile and looked at the various flavors of the toolkit – TensorFlow for Mobile and TensorFlow Lite. We also explored the architecture of a TensorFlow-ML-enabled mobile application. Then we discussed the architecture and details of TensorFlow Lite and its components, and even demonstrated a simple use case for an android mobile application using TensorFlow for mobile.

In the next chapter, we will be using the TensorFlow for mobile that we discussed here to implement a classification algorithm.

Regression Using Core ML in iOS

5

This chapter will provide you with an overview of regression algorithms and insights into the basics of Core ML, and will introduce you to creating a machine learning program leveraging a regression algorithm and predicting the housing price for a given set of housing-related data using Core ML in iOS.

As we already saw in Chapter 1, *Introduction to Machine Learning on Mobile,* any machine learning program has four phases. We will see what we are going to cover in the four phases and what tools we are going to use to solve the underlying machine learning problem.

Problem definition: The housing information of a certain area is provided and we want to predict the median value of a home in this area.

We will be covering the following topics in the chapter:

- Understanding what regression is and how to apply it to solve an ML problem
- Understanding regression using a sample dataset and Excel
- Understanding the basics of Core ML
- Solving the problem using regression in Core ML:
    - Technical requirements
    - How to create the model file using scikit-learn
    - Testing the model
    - Understanding how to import the scikit-learn model into the Core ML project
    - Writing an iOS mobile application and using the scikit-learn model in it and doing the housing price prediction

Introduction to regression

Regression analysis is a basic method used in the statistical analysis of data. It's a statistical method that helps to find the relationships between variables. It is basically used for understanding the relationship between input and output numerical variables. We should first identify the dependent variable, which will vary based on the value of the independent variable. For example, the value of the house (dependent variable) varies based on the square footage of the house (independent variable). Regression analysis is very useful for prediction.

In a simple regression problem (a single x and a single y), the form of the model would be as follows:

$$y = A + B^*x$$

In higher dimensions, when we have more than one input (x), the line is called a **plane** or a **hyperplane**.

In our example, we predict the price of the house based on the various parameters that may impact the price of the data in that particular area.

The following are some of the important points to be considered while addressing a regression problem:

- The prediction is to be a numeric quantity.
- The input variables can be real-valued or discrete.
- If there are multiple input variables then it is called a **multivariate regression problem**.
- When the input variables are ordered by time, the regression problem is called a **time series forecasting problem**.
- Regression should not be confused with classification. Classification is the task of predicting a discrete class label, whereas regression is the task of predicting a continuous quantity.

An algorithm that is capable of learning a regression predictive model is called a **regression algorithm**.

Linear regression

In this section, we will try to understand linear regression using a detailed example with a specific dataset. We are going to use the same dataset to work out the iOS Core ML example too.

Dataset

We will use the Boston dataset for the regression problem. This dataset contains information collected by the US Census Service concerning housing in the area of Boston, Massachusetts. It was obtained from the StatLib archive (`http://lib.stat.cmu.edu/datasets/boston`) and has been used extensively throughout the literature to benchmark algorithms. The dataset is small in size, with only 506 cases.

Dataset naming

The name for this dataset is simply **Boston**. It has two photo tasks: now, in which the nitrous oxide level is to be predicted; and price, in which the median value of a home is to be predicted.

Miscellaneous details about the dataset are as follows:

- **Origin**: The origin of the Boston housing data is Natural.
- **Usage**: This dataset may be used for assessment.
- **Number of cases**: The dataset contains a total of 506 cases.
- **Order**: The order of the cases is mysterious.
- **Variables**: There are 14 attributes in each case of the dataset. They are the following:
    - **CRIM**: Per capita crime rate by town
    - **ZN**: A proportion of residential land zoned for lots over 25,000 sq.ft
    - **INDUS**: A proportion of nonretail business acres per town
    - **CHAS**: Charles River dummy variable (1 if tract bounds river; 0 otherwise)
    - **NOX**: Nitric oxide concentration (parts per 10 million)
    - **RM**: Average number of rooms per dwelling

- **AGE**: A proportion of owner-occupied units built prior to 1940
- **DIS**: Weighted distances to five Boston employment centers
- **RAD**: Index of accessibility to radial highways
- **TAX**: Full-value property-tax rate per $10,000
- **PTRATIO**: Pupil-teacher ratio by a town
- **B**: `1000(Bk - 0.63)^2` where `Bk` is the proportion of blacks by a town
- **LSTAT**: Percentage lower status of the population
- **MEDV**: A median value of owner-occupied homes in $1000

We will try out both simple linear regression as well as multivariate regression using Excel for the dataset and understand the details. We will consider only the following 20 data elements from the 506 sample data space from the Boston dataset for our analysis purposes:

CRIM	ZN	INDUS	CHAS	NOX	RM	AGE	DIS	RAD	TAX	PT	B	LSTAT	MV
0.00632	18	2.309999943	0	0.537999988	6.574999809	65.19999695	4.090000153	1	296	15.3	396.899994	4.980000019	24
0.027310001	0	7.070000172	0	0.469000012	6.421000004	78.90000153	4.967100143	2	242	17.799999	396.899994	9.140000343	21.6
0.02729	0	7.070000172	0	0.469000012	7.184999943	61.09999847	4.967100143	2	242	17.799999	392.829987	4.03000021	34.700001
0.032370001	0	2.180000067	0	0.458000004	6.998000145	45.79999924	6.062200069	3	222	18.700001	394.630005	2.940000057	33.400002
0.069049999	0	2.180000067	0	0.458000004	7.146999836	54.20000076	6.062200069	3	222	18.700001	396.899994	5.329999924	36.200001
0.029850001	0	2.180000067	0	0.458000004	6.429999828	58.70000076	6.062200069	3	222	18.700001	394.119995	5.210000038	28.700001
0.088289998	12.5	7.869999886	0	0.523999989	6.012000084	66.59999847	5.560500145	5	311	15.2	395.600006	12.43000031	22.9
0.144549996	12.5	7.869999886	0	0.523999989	6.171999931	96.09999847	5.950500011	5	311	15.2	396.899994	19.14999962	27.1
0.211239994	12.5	7.869999886	0	0.523999989	5.631000042	100	6.082099915	5	311	15.2	386.630005	29.93000031	16.5
0.170039997	12.5	7.869999886	0	0.523999989	6.004000187	85.90000153	6.592100143	5	311	15.2	386.709992	17.10000038	18.9
0.224889994	12.5	7.869999886	0	0.523999989	6.376999855	94.30000305	6.346700191	5	311	15.2	392.519989	20.45000076	15
0.117470004	12.5	7.869999886	0	0.523999989	6.008999825	82.90000153	6.226699829	5	311	15.2	396.899994	13.27000046	18.9
0.093780003	12.5	7.869999886	0	0.523999989	5.888999939	39	5.450900078	5	311	15.2	390.5	15.71000004	21.700001
0.629760027	0	8.140000343	0	0.537999988	5.948999882	61.79999924	4.707499981	4	307	21	396.899994	8.260000229	20.4
0.637960017	0	8.140000343	0	0.537999988	6.096000195	84.5	4.461900234	4	307	21	380.019989	10.26000023	18.200001
0.627390027	0	8.140000343	0	0.537999988	5.834000111	56.5	4.498600006	4	307	21	395.619995	8.470000267	19.9
1.053930044	0	8.140000343	0	0.537999988	5.934999943	29.29999924	4.498600006	4	307	21	386.850006	6.579999924	23.1
0.784200013	0	8.140000343	0	0.537999988	5.989999771	81.69999695	4.257900238	4	307	21	386.75	14.67000008	17.5
0.802709997	0	8.140000343	0	0.537999988	5.455999851	36.59999847	3.796499968	4	307	21	288.98999	11.68999958	20.200001
0.725799978	0	8.140000343	0	0.53799988	5.727000237	69.5	3.796499968	4	307	21	390.950012	11.27999973	18.200001

Now, we can use the data analysis option given in Excel and try to predict the MV considering the dependent variable DIS alone. In data analysis, select Regression and select the MV as the Y value and DIS as the X value. This is a simple regression with one dependent variable to predict the output. The following is the output produced by Excel:

SUMMARY OUTPUT

Regression Statistics	
Multiple R	0.15842429
R Square	0.02509826
Adjusted R Square	-0.0322489
Standard Error	6.2924382
Observations	19

ANOVA

	df	SS	MS	F	Significance F
Regression	1	17.32884216	17.32884	0.4376547	0.5171238
Residual	17	673.1112344	39.59478		
Total	18	690.4400765			

	Coefficients	Standard Error	t Stat	P-value	Lower 95%	Upper 95%	Lower 95.0%	Upper 95.0%
Intercept	17.1776841	9.067764021	1.894368	0.0753179	-1.9536257	36.30899	-1.953626	36.308994
DIS	1.11806988	1.690063931	0.661555	0.5171238	-2.4476533	4.683793	-2.447653	4.6837931

The linear regression equation for prediction of MV with DIS as the dependent variable would be $Y = 1.11X + 17.17$ (DIS coefficient of DIS + intercept value):

$$R2 = 0.0250$$

Now, we can see the predicted output of MV for the set of 20 data samples considered for analysis:

RESIDUAL OUTPUT				PROBABILITY OUTPUT	
Observation		Predicted MV	Residuals	Percentile	MV
	1	21.75059006	2.249409935	2.631578947	15
	2	22.73124914	-1.131248764	7.894736842	16.5
	3	22.73124914	11.96875162	13.15789474	17.5
	4	23.95564738	9.444354146	18.42105263	18.20000076
	5	23.95564738	12.24435338	23.68421053	18.89999962
	6	23.95564738	4.744353376	28.94736842	18.89999962
	7	23.39471181	-0.494712192	34.21052632	19.89999962
	8	23.83075891	3.269241466	39.47368421	20.20000076
	9	23.9778968	-7.477896803	44.73684211	20.39999962
	10	24.5481127	-5.648113076	50	21.60000038
	11	24.2737384	-9.273738401	55.26315789	21.70000076
	12	24.13956961	-5.239569991	60.52631579	22.89999962
	13	23.27217128	-1.572170518	65.78947368	23.10000038
	14	22.44099802	-2.040998402	71.05263158	24
	15	22.16640034	-3.966399583	76.31578947	27.10000038
	16	22.20743325	-2.307433632	81.57894737	28.70000076
	17	22.20743325	0.892567128	86.84210526	33.40000153
	18	21.93831409	-4.438314092	92.10526316	34.70000076
	19	21.42243635	-1.222435588	97.36842105	36.20000076

The output chart for the MV predicted for the DIS as a dependent variable is given as follows:

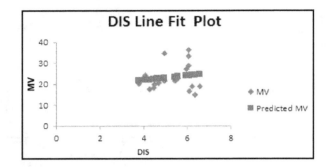

Now, we get an understanding of how linear regression works for a single, dependent variable. In the same way, we can have any number of dependent variables, by including them as *X1, X2, X3, ... XN*.

In our dataset, we have 14 variables in total and we can have the MV dependent on all the remaining 13 variables and create the regression equation in the same manner as specified previously for a single variable.

Now that we have understood how to perform regression for our Boston dataset using Excel, we will be performing the same using Core ML. Before going ahead and implementing in Core ML, we will must understand what Core ML is and look into the basics of Core ML.

Understanding the basics of Core ML

Core ML enables iOS mobile applications to run machine learning models locally on a mobile device. It enables developers to integrate a broad variety of machine learning model types into a mobile application. Developers do not require extensive knowledge of machine learning or deep learning to write machine learning mobile applications using Core ML. They just need to know how to include the ML model into the mobile app similar to other resources and use invoke it in the mobile application. A data scientist or a machine learning expert can create an ML model in any technology they are familiar with, say Keras, scikit-learn, and so on. Core ML provides tools to convert the ML data model created using other tools (tensor, scikit-learn, and so on) to a format that is mandated by Core ML.

This conversion to a Core ML model happens during the app development phase. It does not happen in real time when the application is being used. The conversion is done by using the `coremltools` Python library. When the app deserializes a Core ML model, it becomes an object having a `prediction` method. Core ML is not really meant for training, just for running pretrained models.

Core ML supports extensive deep learning capabilities with support for more than 30 layers. The layers in deep learning actually suggest the number of layers through which the data is transformed. It also supports standard models: tree ensembles, SVMs, and linear models. It is built on top of low-level technologies such as Metal. Core ML seamlessly takes advantage of the CPU and GPU to provide maximum performance and efficiency. It has the ability to switch between CPU and GPU based on the intensity of the task at hand. Since Core ML lets machine learning run locally on the device, data doesn't need to leave the device to be analyzed.

With Core ML, we can integrate trained machine learning models into our app:

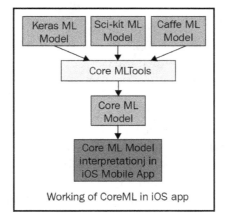

A trained model is the result of applying a machine learning algorithm to a set of training data. The model makes predictions based on new input data. For example, a model that's been trained in a region's historical house prices may be able to predict a house's price when given the number of bedrooms and bathrooms.

Core ML is optimized for on-device performance, which minimizes memory footprint and power consumption. Running strictly on the device ensures the privacy of user data and guarantees that our app remains functional and responsive when a network connection is unavailable.

Core ML is the foundation for domain-specific frameworks and functionality. Core ML supports **Vision** for image analysis, Foundation for **natural language processing,** and **Gameplaykit** for evaluating learned decision trees. **Core ML** itself builds on top of low-level primitives such as **Accelerate** and **BNNS**, as well as **Metal Performance Shaders**:

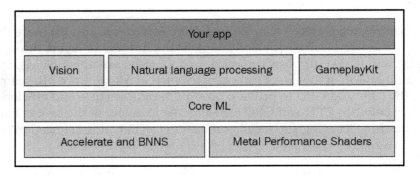

An iOS developer who is going to write ML programs using Core ML needs to be aware of the following fundamental steps:

1. Create the model outside of iOS. This can be done using scikit-learn, TensorFlow, or in any other way with which the developer is comfortable. Create the machine learning model file. For creating the machine learning model file, they need to be aware of the four key phases of machine learning already discussed.
2. Once the model is built, tested, and ready for use, this model needs to be converted to a format that is compatible with Core ML. Core ML tools are available that actually help to convert the model file created using any tool to a model file that is in a format as mandated by Core ML (.mlmodel file format).
3. Once the Core ML specific model file is created, the same can be imported into the iOS program and the Core ML-provided APIs can be used to interact with the model file to extract the required information as may be required by the iOS application, basically importing the .mlmodel file into the resources folder of the Xcode project.

Core ML's biggest advantage is that it is extremely simple to use. Just a few lines of code can help to integrate a complete ML model. Core ML can only help to integrate pretrained ML models into an application. No model training is possible.

Solving the problem using regression in Core ML

This section will go through the details of creating a regression model and then using the regression model in an iOS mobile application. It will provide a detailed walk-through of the various steps involved in creating an iOS regression ML application to address the problem defined.

Technical requirements

The following software needs to be installed on the developer machine:

- Python
- Xcode in a Mac environment

The exercise programs for this chapter can be downloaded from our GitHub repository at `https://github.com/PacktPublishing/Machine-Learning-for-Mobile/tree/master/housing%20price%20prediction`.

In the following program, we are going to use `pandas`, `numpy`, and `scikit-learn` to create the model. So, install these packages from the `pip` package manager using the following command from the Command Prompt/Terminal:

```
pip install scikit-learn
pip install numpy
pip install pandas
```

In order to convert the created model to the Core ML format, we need to use the Core ML `scikit-learn` Python converter provided by Apple:

```
pip install -U coremltools
```

How to create the model file using scikit-learn

This section will explain how we are going to create the linear regression model file using `scikit-learn` and also convert it into the `.mlmodel` file that is compatible with Core ML. We are going to use the Boston dataset for the model creation. The following is a simple Python program, which creates a simple linear regression model using `scikit-learn` using the Boston dataset. Then the Core ML tools convert it into the model file compatible with Core ML. Let's go through the program in detail.

First, we need to import the required packages needed for the program:

```
# importing required packages
import numpy as np
```

The preceding lines import the NumPy package. NumPy is the fundamental package for scientific computing with Python. It contains a powerful N-dimensional array object. This `numpy` array will be used in this program for storing the dataset, which has 14 dimensions:

```
import pandas as pd
from pandas.core import series
```

The preceding line imports the `pandas` package, an open source, BSD-licensed library providing high-performance, easy-to-use data structures and data analysis tools for the Python programming language. Using pandas, we can create a data frame. You can assume a `pandas` data frame as an Excel spreadsheet in which every sheet has headings and data:

```
import coremltools
from coremltools.converters.sklearn import _linear_regression
```

The preceding lines import the Core ML Tools conversion package for the linear regression model that we have used in this program. Core ML Tools is a Python package for creating, examining, and testing models in the `.mlmodel` format. In particular, it can be used to do the following:

- Convert existing models to the `.mlmodel` format from popular machine learning tools including `Keras`, `Caffe`, `scikit-learn`, `libsvm`, and `XGBoost`
- Express models in `.mlmodel` format through a simple API
- Make predictions with an `.mlmodel` (on select platforms for testing purposes):

```
from sklearn import datasets, linear_model
from sklearn.metrics import mean_squared_error, r2_score
```

The preceding lines import the `sklearn` packages. Data sets are used to import built-in datasets in the `sklearn` package. In this program, we are using the Boston housing price dataset that was explained in the previous section. The `linear_model` package is used to get access to the linear regression function, and the metrics package is used to calculate the testing metrics of our model, such as the mean squared error:

```
boston = datasets.load_boston()
```

The preceding line loads the Boston dataset from the `sklearn` datasets package:

```
bos = pd.DataFrame(boston.data)
```

Now, from the entire dataset, we need to extract the data:

```
bos.columns = boston.feature_names
```

Get the column names, that is, the headings for that data:

```
bos['price'] = boston.target
```

Now, let's define the target column that we want to predict. The column defined as the target will be the one that will be predicted:

```
x = bos.drop('price', axis=1)
```

Once we define the target column, we will remove the data from the target column, so that it becomes x:

```
y = bos.price
```

Since we defined price as the target column, `y` is the price column in the dataset's data:

```
X_train,X_test,Y_train,Y_test =
sklearn.model_selection.train_test_split(x,y,test_size=0.3,random_state=5)
```

We then split the data into training and test data as per the 70/30 rule:

```
lm = sklearn.linear_model.LinearRegression()
```

Once we have the training and test data, we can initiate a linear regression object:

```
lm.fit(X_train, Y_train)
```

With the linear regression object that has been initialized, we just have to feed the training and the test data into the regression model:

```
Y_pred = lm.predict(X_test)
```

The preceding line predicts the target:

```
mse = sklearn.metrics.mean_squared_error(Y_test, Y_pred)
print(mse);
```

The preceding lines will calculate the mean squared error in our fitted model and predicted results.

Because a regression predictive model predicts a quantity, the skill of the model must be reported as an error in those predictions.

There are many ways to estimate the skill of a regression predictive model, but the most common is to calculate the **root mean squared error** (**RMSE**).

For example, if a regression predictive model made two predictions, one of *1.5* where the expected value is *1.0* and another of 3.3 and the expected value is *3.0*, then the *RMSE* would be as follows:

1	*RMSE = sqrt(average(error^2))*
2	*RMSE = sqrt(((1.0 - 1.5)^2 + (3.0 - 3.3)^2) / 2)*
3	*RMSE = sqrt((0.25 + 0.09) / 2)*
4	*RMSE = sqrt(0.17)*
5	*RMSE = 0.412*

A benefit of *RMSE* is that the units of the error score are in the same units as the predicted value:

```
model = coremltools.converters.sklearn.convert(
    sk_obj=lm, input_features=boston.feature_names,
    output_feature_names='price')
```

In the preceding line, we are converting the fitted model to the Core ML format. Basically, this is the line where the `.mlmodel` file is created. And we are also specifying the input and output column names:

```
model.save('HousePricer.mlmodel')
```

In the preceding line, we are saving the model to the disk. This can later be used in our iOS program.

Running and testing the model

When the model created by `scikit-learn` was executed and tested independently before converting it into the Core ML format, the following variance and mean square error were found:

- The mean square error for the prepared model was `30.703232`
- The variance score was `0.68`
- The process finished with exit code `0`

The following graph gives an idea of the predicted values versus the actual values:

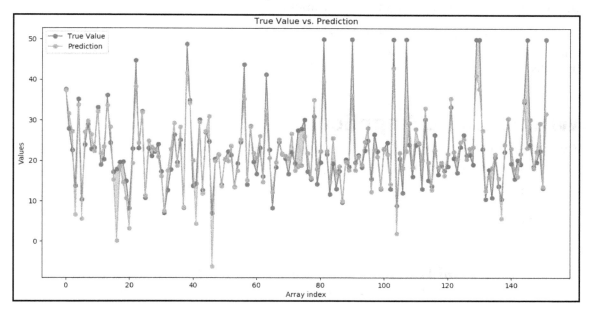

Importing the model into the iOS project

The following is the project structure of the Xcode project where the `.mlmodel` file is imported and used for prediction:

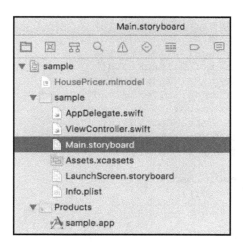

The `ViewCcontroller.swift` file is where the model file created is used and the housing prediction is carried out in a mobile application.

The `housePricer.mlmodel` file is the model file that was created using `scikit-learn` and converted into the ML model file using the Core ML converter tools. This file is included in the `resources` folder of the iOS Xcode project.

Writing the iOS application

This section provides the details of the `Swift` code that uses the model in the `.mlmodel` format and does the housing price prediction:

```
//  ViewController.swift
import UIKit
import CoreML
class ViewController: UIViewController {
    let model = HousePricer()
```

This line is to initialize the model class that we have imported into the project. The following lines define outlets/variables to the text fields to interact with them:

```
@IBOutlet weak var crim: UITextField!
@IBOutlet weak var zn: UITextField!
@IBOutlet weak var price: UILabel!
@IBOutlet weak var b: UITextField!
@IBOutlet weak var ptratio: UITextField!
@IBOutlet weak var medv: UITextField!
@IBOutlet weak var lstat: UITextField!
@IBOutlet weak var rad: UITextField!
@IBOutlet weak var tax: UITextField!
@IBOutlet weak var dis: UITextField!
@IBOutlet weak var age: UITextField!
@IBOutlet weak var rm: UITextField!
@IBOutlet weak var nox: UITextField!
@IBOutlet weak var chas: UITextField!
@IBOutlet weak var indus: UITextField!
override func didReceiveMemoryWarning() {
    super.didReceiveMemoryWarning()
    // Dispose of any resources that can be recreated.
}
override func viewDidLoad() {
    super.viewDidLoad();
    updated(rad);
}
@IBAction func updated(_ sender: Any) {
```

```
        guard let modeloutput = try? model.prediction(CRIM:
Double(crim.text!)!, ZN: Double(zn.text!)!, INDUS: Double(indus.text!)!,
CHAS: Double(chas.text!)!, NOX: Double(nox.text!)!, RM: Double(rm.text!)!,
AGE: Double(age.text!)!, DIS: Double(dis.text!)!, RAD: Double(rad.text!)!,
TAX: Double(tax.text!)!, PTRATIO: Double(ptratio.text!)!, B:
Double(b.text!)!, LSTAT: Double(lstat.text!)!) else {
            fatalError("unexpected runtime error")
    }
        price.text = "$" + String(format: "%.2f",modeloutput.price);
    }
}
```

The preceding function is added as an `onchange` listener to all the preceding text fields. In this, we are using the model object we have created previously and predicting the price for the given values in the text fields.

Running the iOS application

The Xcode project created was executed in the simulator and the following is the sample we got:

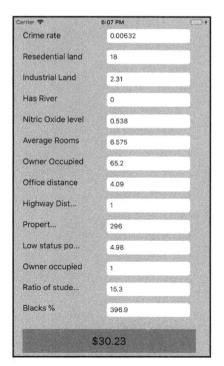

Further reading

We can get more insight into Core ML and the services it offers by going to its official website at https://developer.apple.com/documentation/coreml.

Summary

In this chapter, we covered the following topics:

- **Linear regression**: Understanding the algorithm and implementing it for the Boston housing dataset using an Excel sheet.
- **Core ML**: We went through the high-level details of Core ML and the various features it offers.
- **A sample application implemented for linear regression using Core ML**: We took the Boston housing dataset and implemented the linear regression model using Core ML for an iOS mobile application and viewed the results in a mobile application.

The ML Kit SDK

6

In this chapter, we will discuss ML Kit, which was announced by Firebase at the Google I/O 2018. This SDK packages Google's mobile machine learning offerings under a single umbrella.

Mobile application developers may want to implement features in their mobile apps that require machine learning capabilities. However, they may not have knowledge of machine learning concepts and which algorithms to use for which scenarios, how to build the model, train the model, and so on.

ML Kit tries to address this problem by identifying all the potential use cases for machine learning in the context of mobile devices, and providing ready-made APIs. If the correct inputs are passed to these, the required output is received, with no further coding required.

Additionally, this kit enables the inputs to be passed either to on-device APIs that work offline, or to online APIs that are hosted in the cloud.

To top it all, ML Kit also provides options for developers with expertise in machine learning, allowing them to build their own models using TensorFlow/TensorFlow Lite, and them import them into the application and invoke them using ML Kit APIs.

ML Kit also offers further useful features, such as model upgrade and monitoring capabilities (if hosted with Firebase).

We will cover the following topics in this chapter:

- ML Kit and its features
- Creating an image-labeling sample using ML Kit on-device APIs
- Creating the same sample using ML Kit cloud APIs
- Creating Face Detection application

Understanding ML Kit

ML Kit encompasses all the existing Google offerings for machine learning on mobile. It bundles the Google Cloud Vision API, TensorFlow Lite, and the Android Neural Networks API together in a single SDK, as shown:

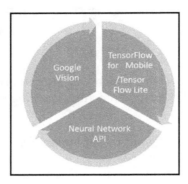

ML Kit enables developers to utilize machine learning in their mobile applications for both Android and iOS apps, in a very easy way. Inference can be carried out by invoking APIs that are either on-device or on-cloud.

The advantages of on-device APIs are that they work completely offline, and are more secure as no data is sent to the cloud. By contrast, on-cloud APIs do require network connectivity, and do send data off-device, but allow for greater accuracy.

ML Kit offers APIs covering the following machine learning scenarios that may be required by mobile application developers:

- Image labeling
- Text recognition
- Landmark detection
- Face detection
- Barcode scanning

All these APIs are implemented using complex machine learning algorithms. However, those details are wrapped. The mobile developer need not get into the details of which algorithms are used for implementing these APIs; all that needs to be done is to pass the desired data to the SDK, and in return the correct output will be received back, depending on which part of ML Kit is being used.

If the provided APIs don't cover a specific use case, you can build your own TensorFlow Lite model. ML Kit will help to host that model, and serve it to your mobile application.

Since Firebase ML Kit provides both on-device and on-cloud capabilities, developers can come up with innovative solutions to leverage either or both, based on the specific problem at hand. All they need to know is that on-device APIs are fast and work offline, while Cloud APIs utilize the Google Cloud platform to provide predictions with increased levels of accuracy.

The following diagram describes the issues to consider when deciding between on-device or on-cloud APIs:

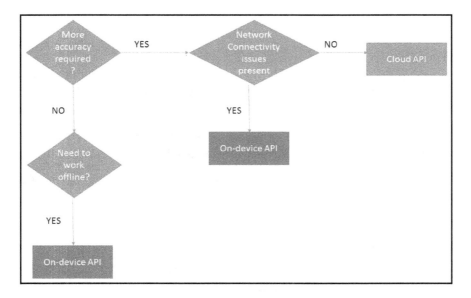

ML Kit APIs

Not all APIs provided by ML Kit are supported in both on-device and on-cloud modes. The following table shows which APIs are supported in each mode:

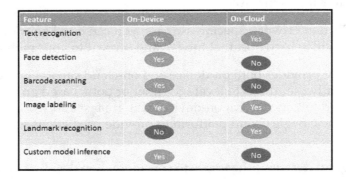

Feature	On-Device	On-Cloud
Text recognition	Yes	Yes
Face detection	Yes	No
Barcode scanning	Yes	No
Image labeling	Yes	Yes
Landmark recognition	No	Yes
Custom model inference	Yes	No

Let's look at the details of each API.

Text recognition

ML Kit's text recognition APIs help with the recognition of text in any Latin-based language, using the mobile device camera. They are available both on-device and on-cloud.

The on-device API allows for recognition of sparse text, or text present in images. The cloud API does the same, but also allows for recognition of bulk text, such as in documents. The cloud API also supports recognition of more languages than device APIs are capable of.

Possible use cases for these APIs would be to recognize text in images, to scan for characters that may be embedded in images, or to automate tedious data entry.

Face detection

The ML Kit's face detection API allows for the detection of faces in an image or video. Once the face is detected, we can apply the following refinements:

- **Landmark detection**: Determining specific points of interest (landmarks) within the face, such as the eyes
- **Classification**: Classifying the face based on certain characteristics, such as whether the eyes are open or closed
- **Face tracking**: Recognizing and tracking the same face (in various positions) across different frames of video

Face detection can be done only on-device and in real time. There may be many use cases for mobile device applications, in which the camera captures an image and manipulates it based on landmarks or classifications, to produce selfies, avatars, and so on.

Barcode scanning

ML Kit's barcode-scanning API helps read data encoded using most standard barcode formats. It supports linear formats such as Codabar, Code 39, Code 93, Code 128, EAN-8, EAN-13, ITF, UPC-A, or UPC-E, as well as 2-D formats such as Aztec, Data Matrix, PDF417, or QR codes.

The API can recognize and scan barcodes regardless of their orientation. Any structured data that is stored as a barcode can be recognized.

Image labeling

ML Kit's image-labeling APIs help recognize entities in an image. There is no need for any other metadata information to be provided for this entity recognition. Image labeling gives insight into the content of images. The ML Kit API provides the entities in the images, along with a confidence score for each one.

Image labeling is available both on-device and on-cloud, with the difference being the number of labels supported. The on-device API supports around 400 labels, while the cloud-based API supports up to 10,000.

Landmark recognition

The ML Kit's landmark recognition API helps recognize well-known landmarks in an image.

This API, when given an image as input, will provide the landmarks found in the image along with geographical coordinates and region information. The knowledge graph entity ID is also returned for the landmark. This ID is a string that uniquely identifies the landmark that was recognized.

Custom model inference

If the APIs provided out-of-the-box are not sufficient for your use case, ML Kit also provides the option to create your own custom model and deploy it through ML Kit.

Creating a text recognition app using Firebase on-device APIs

To get started in ML Kit, you need to sign in to your Google account, activate your Firebase account, and create a Firebase project. Follow these steps:

- Go to `https://firebase.google.com/`.
- Sign in to your Google account, if you are not already signed in.
- Click **Go to console** in the menu bar.
- Click **Add project** to create a project and open it.

Now open Android Studio, and create a project with an empty activity. Note down the app package name that you have given while creating the project—for example, `com.packt.mlkit.textrecognizationondevice`.

Next, go to the Firebase console. In the **Project overview** menu, click **Add app** and give the required information. It will give you a JSON file to download. Add to the app folder of your project in project view in Android Studio, as shown in the following screenshot:

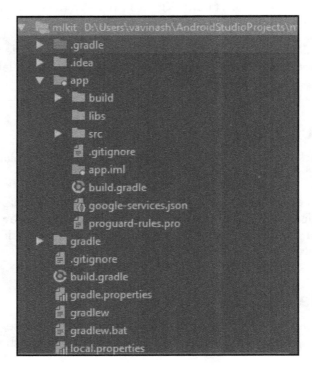

Next, add the following lines of code to the manifest file:

```
<uses-feature android:name="android.hardware.camera2.full" /<
<uses-permission android:name="android.permission.CAMERA" /<
<uses-permission android:name="android.permission.INTERNET" /<
<uses-permission android:name="android.permission.WRITE_EXTERNAL_STORAGE"
/<
<uses-permission android:name="android.permission.READ_EXTERNAL_STORAGE" /<
```

We need these permissions for our app to work. The next line tells the Firebase
dependencies to download the **text recognition** (**OCR**) model from the Google server, and
keep it in the device for inference:

```
<meta-data
    android:name="com.google.firebase.ml.vision.DEPENDENCIES"
    android:value="ocr" /<
```

The whole manifest file will look as follows:

```
<?xml version="1.0" encoding="utf-8"?<
<manifest xmlns:android="http://schemas.android.com/apk/res/android"
    package="com.packt.mlkit.testrecognizationondevice"<

    <uses-feature android:name="android.hardware.camera2.full" /<
    <uses-permission android:name="android.permission.CAMERA" /<
    <uses-permission android:name="android.permission.INTERNET" /<
    <uses-permission
android:name="android.permission.WRITE_EXTERNAL_STORAGE" /<
    <uses-permission
android:name="android.permission.READ_EXTERNAL_STORAGE" /<
    <application
        android:allowBackup="true"
        android:icon="@mipmap/ic_launcher"
        android:label="@string/app_name"
        android:roundIcon="@mipmap/ic_launcher_round"
        android:supportsRtl="true"
        android:theme="@style/AppTheme"<

        <meta-data
            android:name="com.google.firebase.ml.vision.DEPENDENCIES"
            android:value="ocr" /<

        <activity android:name=".MainActivity"<
            <intent-filter<
                <action android:name="android.intent.action.MAIN" /<

                <category android:name="android.intent.category.LAUNCHER"
```

```
/<
            </intent-filter<
        </activity<
    </application<

</manifest<
```

Now, we need to add the Firebase dependencies to the project. To do so, we need to add the following lines to the project `build.gradle` file:

```
buildscript {
    repositories {
        google()
        jcenter()
    }
    dependencies {
        classpath 'com.android.tools.build:gradle:3.1.4' //this version
will defer dependeds on your environment.
        classpath 'com.google.gms:google-services:4.0.1'

        // NOTE: Do not place your application dependencies here; they
belong
        // in the individual module build.gradle files
    }
}
```

Then open the module app `build.gradle` file, and add the following dependencies:

```
implementation 'com.google.firebase:firebase-ml-vision:17.0.0'
implementation 'com.google.firebase:firebase-core:16.0.3'
```

Also add the following line to the bottom of that file:

```
apply plugin: 'com.google.gms.google-services'
```

Now, in your layout file, write the following `.xml` code to define the elements:

```
<?xml version="1.0" encoding="utf-8"?<
<RelativeLayout xmlns:android="http://schemas.android.com/apk/res/android"
    xmlns:tools="http://schemas.android.com/tools"
    android:layout_width="match_parent"
    android:layout_height="match_parent"
    tools:context=" (main activity)"< <!-- Here your fully qualified main
activity class name will come. --<

    <TextureView
        android:id="@+id/preview"
        android:layout_width="match_parent"
```

```
    android:layout_height="wrap_content"
    android:layout_above="@id/btn_takepic"
    android:layout_alignParentTop="true"/<

<Button
    android:id="@+id/btn_takepic"
    android:layout_width="wrap_content"
    android:layout_height="wrap_content"
    android:layout_alignParentBottom="true"
    android:layout_centerHorizontal="true"
    android:layout_marginBottom="16dp"
    android:layout_marginTop="16dp"
    android:text="Start Labeling"
    /<
</RelativeLayout<
```

Now, it's time to code your application's main activity class.

Please download the application code from Packt Github repository at https://github. com/PacktPublishing/Machine-Learning-for-Mobile/tree/master/mlkit

We are assuming you are already familiar with Android—so, we are discussing the code using Firebase functionalities:

```
import com.google.firebase.FirebaseApp;
import com.google.firebase.ml.vision.FirebaseVision;
import com.google.firebase.ml.vision.common.FirebaseVisionImage;
import com.google.firebase.ml.vision.text.FirebaseVisionTextRecognizer;
import com.google.firebase.ml.vision.text.*;
```

The preceding code will import the firebase libraries.

```
private FirebaseVisionTextRecognizer textRecognizer;
```

The preceding line will declare the firebase text recognizer.

```
FirebaseApp fapp= FirebaseApp.initializeApp(getBaseContext());
```

The preceding line will initialize the Firebase application context.

```
        textRecognizer =
FirebaseVision.getInstance().getOnDeviceTextRecognizer();
```

The preceding line will get the on-device text recognizer.

```
takePictureButton.setOnClickListener(new View.OnClickListener() {
    @Override
    public void onClick(View v) {
        takePicture();
        //In this function we are having the code to decode the
characters in the picture
    }
});
}
```

The preceding code snippet registers the on-click-event listener for the take-picture button.

```
Bitmap bmp = BitmapFactory.decodeByteArray(bytes,0,bytes.length);
```

Creating a bitmap from the byte array.

```
FirebaseVisionImage firebase_image = FirebaseVisionImage.fromBitmap(bmp);
```

The preceding line creates a firebase image object to pass through the recognizer.

```
textRecognizer.processImage(firebase_image)
```

The preceding line passes the created image object to the recognizer for processing.

```
.addOnSuccessListener(new OnSuccessListener<FirebaseVisionText<() {
                            @Override
                            public void
onSuccess(FirebaseVisionText result) {
//On receiving the results displaying to the user.
Toast.makeText(getApplicationContext(),result.getText(),Toast.LENGTH_LONG).
show();
                                    }
                            })
```

The preceding code block will add the on-success listener. It will receive a firebase vision text object, which it in turn displays to the user in the form of a `Toast` message.

```
.addOnFailureListener(
        new OnFailureListener() {
            @Override
            public void onFailure(@NonNull Exception e)
                {
                        Toast.makeText(getApplicationContext(),"Unable to
read the text",Toast.LENGTH_LONG).show();
                }
            });
```

The preceding code block will add the `on-failure` listener. It will receive an exception object, which is in turn a display error message to the user in the form of a `Toast` message.

When you run the preceding code, you will have the following output in your device:

Note that you must be connected to the internet while installing this app, as Firebase needs to download the model to your device.

Creating a text recognition app using Firebase on-cloud APIs

In this section, we are going to convert the on-device app to a cloud app. The difference is that on-device apps download the model and store it on the device. This allows for a lower inference time, allowing the app to make quick predictions.

By contrast, cloud-based apps upload the image to the Google server, meaning inference will happen there. It won't work if you are not connected to the internet.

In this case, why use a cloud-based model? Because on-device, the model has limited space and processing hardware, whereas Google's servers are scalable. The Google on-cloud text recognizer model is also able to decode multiple languages.

To get started, you need a Google Cloud subscription. Follow these steps:

- Go to your Firebase project console
- In the menu on the left, you will see that you are currently on the Spark Plan (the free tier)
- Click **Upgrade**, and follow the instructions to upgrade to the Blaze Plan, which is pay-as-you-go
- You need to provide credit card or payment details for verification purposes—these will not be charged automatically
- Once you subscribe, you will receive 1,000 Cloud Vision API requests free each month

 This program can be tried only if you have a upgraded Blaze Plan and not a free tier account. The steps are given to create a upgraded account and please follow steps to get the account to try the program given.

By default, Cloud Vision is not enabled for your project. To do so, you need to go to the following link: `https://console.cloud.google.com/apis/library/vision.googleapis.com/?authuser=0`. In the top menu dropdown, select the Firebase project containing the Android app you added in the previous section.

Click **Enable** to enable this feature for your app. The page will look like the following screenshot:

Now return to your code, and make the following changes.

You can find the application code in our Packt Github repository at: `https://github.com/PacktPublishing/Machine-Learning-for-Mobile/tree/master/Testrecognizationoncloud`.

All the other files, except the main activity, have no changes.

The changes are as follows:

```
import com.google.firebase.FirebaseApp;
import com.google.firebase.ml.vision.FirebaseVision;
import com.google.firebase.ml.vision.common.FirebaseVisionImage;
import com.google.firebase.ml.vision.document.FirebaseVisionDocumentText;
import com.google.firebase.ml.vision.document.FirebaseVisionDocumentTextRecognizer;
```

Now, we need to import the preceding packages as dependencies.

```
private FirebaseVisionDocumentTextRecognizer textRecognizer;
```

The preceding code will declare the document text recognizer.

```
textRecognizer =
FirebaseVision.getInstance().getCloudDocumentTextRecognizer();
```

The preceding code instantiates and assigns the cloud text recognizer.

```
takePictureButton.setOnClickListener(new View.OnClickListener() {
    @Override
    public void onClick(View v) {
        takePicture();
        //In this function we are having the code to decode the
characters in the picture
    }
});
}
```

The preceding code registers the on-click-event listener for the take-picture button.

```
Bitmap bmp = BitmapFactory.decodeByteArray(bytes,0,bytes.length);
```

The preceding line creates a bitmap from the byte array.

```
FirebaseVisionImage firebase_image = FirebaseVisionImage.fromBitmap(bmp);
```

The preceding line creates a firebase image object to pass through the recognizer.

```
textRecognizer.processImage(firebase_image)
```

The preceding line passes the created image object to the recognizer for processing.

```
.addOnSuccessListener(new OnSuccessListener<FirebaseVisionDocumentText<() {
    @Override
    public void
onSuccess(FirebaseVisionDocumentText result) {
Toast.makeText(getApplicationContext(),result.getText(),Toast.LENGTH_LONG).
show();
    }
})
```

The preceding code block will add the on-success listener. It will receive a FirebaseVision document text object, which is in turn displayed to the user in the form of a `Toast` message.

```
.addOnFailureListener(
    new OnFailureListener() {
        @Override
        public void onFailure(@NonNull Exception e)
        {
            Toast.makeText(getApplicationContext(),"Unable to
```

```
read the text",Toast.LENGTH_LONG).show();
                  }
         });
```

The preceding code block will add the on-failure listener. It will receive an exception object, which is in turn a display error message to the user in the form of a `Toast` message.

```
Once you run the code with the internet-connected device , you will get the
same output as before, but from the cloud.
```

Face detection using ML Kit

Now we will try to understand how face detection works with ML Kit. Face detection, which was previously part of the Mobile Vision API, has now been moved to ML Kit.

Face detection concepts

The Google Developers page defines face detection as the process of automatically locating and detecting human faces in visual media (digital images or video). The detected face is reported at a position with an associated size and orientation. After the face is detected, we can search for landmarks present in the face such as the eyes and nose.

Here are some important terms to understand before we can move on to programming face detection with ML Kit:

- **Face Orientation**: Detects faces at a range of different angles.
- **Face Recognition**: Determines whether two faces can belong to the same person.
- **Face Tracking**: Refers to detecting faces in videos.
- **Landmark**: Refers to a point of interest within a face. This corresponds to the notable features on a face, such as the right eye, left eye, and nose base.
- **Classification**: Determines the presence of facial characteristics, such as open or closed eye or a smiling or serious face.

Sample solution for face detection using ML Kit

Now open Android Studio, and create a project with an empty activity. Note down the app package name that you have given while creating the project—for example, `com.packt.mlkit.facerecognization`.

Here we are going to modify the text recognition code to predict faces. So, we are not changing the package names and other things. Just the code changes. The project structure is the same as shown previously:

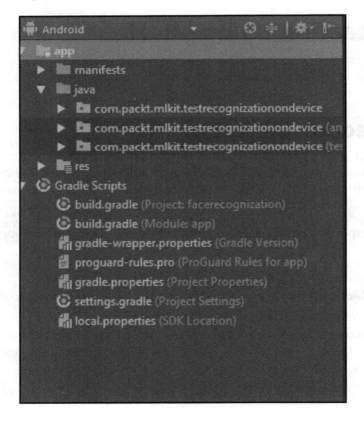

It's time to code our application's main activity class. First we need to download the application code from the Packt GitHub repository at `https://github.com/PacktPublishing/Machine-Learning-for-Mobile/tree/master/facerecognization`. and open the project in Android Studio.

Then we will add the following lines of code to the Gradle dependencies. Open the `build.gradle` file of the module app and add the following dependencies:

```
implementation 'com.google.android.gms:play-services-vision:11.4.0'
implementation 'com.android.support.constraint:constraint-layout:1.0.2'
```

Now we will add the import statements to work with face detection:

```
import com.google.android.gms.vision.Frame;
import com.google.android.gms.vision.face.Face;
import com.google.android.gms.vision.face.FaceDetector;
```

The following statement will declare the `FaceDetector` object:

```
private FaceDetector detector;
```

Now we will create an object and assign it to the declared detector:

```
detector = new FaceDetector.Builder(getApplicationContext())
  .setTrackingEnabled(false)
  .setLandmarkType(FaceDetector.ALL_LANDMARKS)
  .setClassificationType(FaceDetector.ALL_CLASSIFICATIONS)
  .build();
```

We declared a string object to save the prediction messages to the user:

```
String scanResults = "";
```

Here we will check whether the detector is operational; we also have a bitmap object that was obtained from the camera:

```
if (detector.isOperational() && bmp != null) {
```

Then we create a frame object, which `FaceDetector` class detect method needs to predict the face information:

```
Frame frame = new Frame.Builder().setBitmap(bmp).build();SparseArray<Face>
faces = detector.detect(frame);
```

Once it successfully detects, it will return the face object array. The following code appends the information that each `nface` object has to our results string:

```
for (int index = 0; index < faces.size(); ++index) {
    Face face = faces.valueAt(index);
    scanResults += "Face " + (index + 1) + "\n";
    scanResults += "Smile probability:" + "\n" ;
    scanResults += String.valueOf(face.getIsSmilingProbability()) + "\n";
scanResults += "Left Eye Open Probability: " + "\n";
    scanResults += String.valueOf(face.getIsLeftEyeOpenProbability()) +
"\n";
    scanResults += "Right Eye Open Probability: " + "\n";
    scanResults += String.valueOf(face.getIsRightEyeOpenProbability()) +
"\n";
}
```

If no faces are returned, then the following error message will be shown:

```
if (faces.size() == 0) {
    scanResults += "Scan Failed: Found nothing to scan";
}
```

If the face size is not 0, that means it already went through the `for` loop, which appended the faces information to our results text. Now we will add the total number of faces and end the result string:

```
else {
    scanResults += "No of Faces Detected: " + "\n";
    scanResults += String.valueOf(faces.size()) +
\n";
    scanResults += "---------" + "\n";
}
```

If the detector is not operational then the error message will be shown to the user as follows:

```
else {
    scanResults += "Could not set up the detector!";
}
```

Finally, the following code will show the results to the reader:

```
Toast.makeText(getApplicationContext(), scanResults, Toast.LENGTH_LONG).show(
);
```

Running the app

Now it's time to run the app. For that, you will have to connect your mobile to your desktop through the USB debugging option in your mobile and install the app:

On running the app, you will have the following as the output:

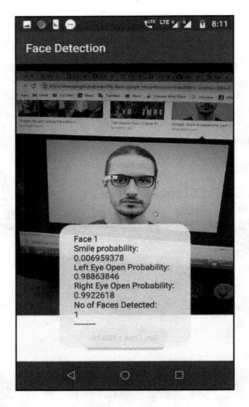

Summary

In this chapter, we discussed ML Kit SDK, which was announced by Firebase at Google I/O 2018. We covered different APIs provided by ML Kit, such as image labeling, text recognition, landmark detection, and more. We then created a text recognition app using on-device APIs, and then using on-cloud APIs. We also create an Face detection application by making minor changes in text recognition application. In the next chapter, we will learn about a spam messages classifier and build a sample implementation of such a classifier for iOS.

Spam Message Detection

This chapter will provide you with an overview of **natural language processing (NLP)** and discuss how NLP can be combined with machine learning to provide solutions to problems. Then, the chapter will take a real-world use case of doing spam message detection by utilizing NLP, combined with the linear SVM classification model. The program will be implemented as a mobile application using Core ML for iOS.

To handle text in machine learning algorithms, we will go through the various NLP techniques that will be used on the text data to make it ready for learning algorithms. Once the text is prepared, we will see how we can classify it using the linear SVM model.

Problem definition: The bulk SMS message data is provided, and these messages need to be classified as spam or non-spam messages.

We will be covering the following topics in this chapter:

- Understanding NLP
- Understanding the linear SVM algorithm
- Solving the problem using linear SVM in Core ML:
    - Technical requirements
    - How to create the model file using scikit-learn
    - Testing the model
    - Importing the scikit-learn model into the Core ML project
    - Writing an iOS mobile application, using the scikit-learn model in it, and doing spam message detection

Understanding NLP

NLP is a huge topic, and it is beyond the scope of this book to go into detail on the subject. However, in this section, we will go through the high-level details of NLP and try to understand the key concepts required to prepare and process the textual data using NLP, in order to make it ready for consumption by machine learning algorithms for prediction.

Introducing NLP

Huge, unstructured textual data is getting generated on a daily basis. Social media, websites such as Twitter and Facebook, and communication apps, such as WhatsApp, generate an enormous volume of this unstructured data daily—not to mention the volume created by blogs, news articles, product reviews, service reviews, advertisements, emails, and SMS. So, to summarize, there is **huge data** (in TBS).

However, it is not possible for a computer to get any insight from this data and to carry out specific actions based on the insights, directly from this huge data, because of the following reasons:

- The data is unstructured
- The data cannot be understood directly without preprocessing
- This data cannot be directly fed in an unprocessed form into any ML algorithms

To make this data more meaningful and to derive information from it, we use NLP. The field of study that focuses on the interactions between human language and computers is called **NLP**. NLP is a branch of data science that is closely related to computational linguistics. It deals with the science of the computer – analyzing, understanding, and deriving information from human natural language-based data, which is usually unstructured like text, speech, and so on.

Through NLP, computers can analyze and derive meaning from human language and do many useful things. By utilizing NLP, many complex tasks, such as an automatic summary of huge documents, translations, relationship extraction between a different mass of unstructured data, sentiment analysis, and speech recognition, can be accomplished.

For computers to understand and analyze human language, we need to analyze the sentence in a more structured manner and understand the core of it. In any sentence, we need to understand three core things:

- **Semantic information**: This relates to the meaning of the sentence. This is the specific meaning of the words in the sentence, for example, *The kite flies*. Here, we don't know whether the kite is man-made or a bird.
- **Syntactic information**: This relates to the structure of the sentence. This is the specific syntactic meaning of the words in a sentence. *Sreeja saw Geetha with candy*. Here, we are not sure who has the candy: Sreeja or Geetha?
- **Pragmatic information (context)**: This relates to the context (linguistic or non-linguistic) of the sentence. This is the specific context in which the words in the sentence are used. For example, *He is out* in the context of baseball and healthcare is different.

However, computers cannot analyze and recognize sentences as humans do. Therefore, there is a well-defined way to enable computers to perform text processing. Here are the main steps involved in that exercise:

1. **Preprocessing**: This step deals with removing all the noise from the sentence, so the only information critical in the context of the sentence is retained for the next step. For example, language stop words ("noise"), such as *is*, *the*, or *an*, can be removed from the sentence for further processing. When processing the sentence, the human brain doesn't take into consideration the noise that's present in the language. Similarly, the computer can be fed with noiseless text for further processing.
2. **Feature engineering**: For the computer to process the preprocessed text, it needs to know the key features of the sentence. This is what is accomplished through the feature engineering step.
3. **NLP processing**: With the human language converted into a feature matrix, the computer can perform NLP processing, which could either be classification, sentiment analysis, or text matching.

Now, let's try to understand the high-level activities that would be performed in each of these steps.

Text-preprocessing techniques

Before we can process text, it needs to be preprocessed. Preprocessing would deal with the following:

- Removing noise from the text under consideration
- Normalizing the sentence
- Standardizing the sentence

There can be additional steps, such as a grammar check or spellcheck, based on the requirements.

Removing noise

Any text present in the sentence that may not be relevant to the context of the data can be termed noise.

For example, this can include language stop words (commonly used words in a language – *is, am, the, of,* and *in*), URLs or links, social media entities (mentions, hashtags), and punctuation.

To remove the noise from the sentence, the general approach is to maintain a dictionary of noise words and then iterate through the tokens of the sentence under consideration against this dictionary and remove matching stop words. The dictionary of noise words is updated frequently to cover all possible noise.

Normalization

The disparities of words in sentences are converted into a normalized form. The words in a sentence may vary, such as *sing, singer, sang,* or *singing*, but they all would more or less fit into the same context and could be standardized.

There are different ways to normalize sentences:

- **Stemming:** A basic rule-based process of stripping the suffixes (*-ing, -ly, -es, -s*) from a word.
- **Lemmatization:** The more sophisticated procedure to identify the root form of a word. It involves a more complex process of verifying the semantics and syntax.

Standardization

This step involves standardizing the sentence to make sure it contains tokens that are from the standard language dictionary only and not anything else, such as hashtags, colloquial words, and so on. All these are removed in this step.

Feature engineering

Now that the text has been processed, the next step to arrange the features from the text so that they can be fed into any machine learning algorithm to carry out classification, clustering, and so on. There are various methods to convert the text into a feature matrix, and we will go through some of them in this section.

Entity extraction

Here, the key entities from the sentence that would be used for NLP processing are extracted. **Named entity recognition** (**NER**) is one such method, where the entities could be named entities, such as that of a place, person, or monument.

Topic modeling

This is another method, where the topics are identified from the corpus of text. The topics can be single words, patterns of words, or sequences of co-occurring words. Based on a number of words in the topic, these could be called **N-Gram.** So, based on context and repeatability, bigrams and trigrams could be used as features.

Bag-of-words model

A bag-of-words model is a representation of text that describes the occurrence of words within a document. It involves the representation of known words and a measure of the presence of known words in the document. The model is more centered around the occurrence of known words in the document, and not about the order of words or the structure of words in the document.

Statistical Engineering

Text data can also be represented as numerical values using various techniques. **Term Frequency-Inverse Document Frequency** (**TF-IDF**) for a huge corpus of text documents is an important technique in this class.

TF–IDF

TF-IDF is a weighted model that's used to convert the text documents into vector models on the basis of the occurrence of words in the documents without considering the exact ordering of text in the document.

Let's consider a set of N text documents and any one document to be D. Then, we define the following.

TF

This measures how frequently a term occurs in a document. Since every document is a different length, it is possible that a term would appear more in long documents than shorter ones. Thus, the TF is often divided by the document length to normalize it:
TF(t) = (Number of times term t appears in a document(D))/(Total number of terms in the document(N)).

Inverse Document Frequency (IDF)

This measures how important a term is for the corpus. While computing TF, all terms are considered equally important. However, it is common thinking that stop words occur more often, but they are less important as far as NLP is concerned. Thus, there is a need to bring down the importance of common terms and bring up the importance of rare terms, hence the IDF, which is calculated as follows:

IDF(t) = log_e(Total number of documents/Number of documents with term t in it)

TF-IDF

The TF IDF formula gives the relative importance of a term in a corpus (list of documents), given by the following formula:

$$w_{i,j} = tf_{i,j} \times log(\frac{N}{df_i})$$

Where:

- $tf_{i,j}$ = number of occurence of i in j
- df_i = number of documents containing i
- N = total number of document

 Consider a document that contains 1,000 words, wherein the word rat appears 3 times. The **term frequency (TF)** for rat is then (3/1000=) 0.003. Now, in 10,000 documents, the word cat appears in 1,000 of them. Therefore, the **inverse document frequency (IDF)** is calculated as log(10000/1000) = 1. Thus, the TF-IDF weight is the product of these quantities is 0.003 * 1 = 0.12.

The words or features in the text corpus could also be organized as feature vectors for easy feeding into the next step of NLP processing.

Classifying/clustering the text

The last step is to actually carry out classification or clustering using the feature engineered matrix or word vectors. We could use any classification algorithm and feed the feature vector to carry out classification or clustering.

Similar to carrying out the clustering, different similarity measures could be used, such as Cosine Distance or Levenshtein distance.

Understanding linear SVM algorithm

In Chapter 2, *Supervised and Unsupervised Learning Algorithms,* we covered the SVM algorithm and now have an idea of how the SVM model works. A linear support vector machine or linear SVM is a linear classifier that tries to find a hyperplane with the largest margin that splits the input space into two regions.

A hyperplane is a generalization of a plane. In one dimension, a hyperplane is called a **point**. In two dimensions, it is a line. In three dimensions, it is a plane. In more dimensions, you can call it a hyperplane.

As we saw, the goal of SVM is to identify the hyperplane that tries to find the largest margin that splits the input space into two regions. If the input space is linearly separable, it is easy to separate them. However, in real life, we find that the input space is very non-linear:

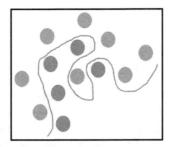

In the preceding scenario, the SVM can help us separate the red and blue balls by using what is called a **Kernel Trick**, which is the method of using a linear classifier to solve a non-linear problem.

The kernel function is applied to each data instance to map the original non-linear observations into a higher-dimensional space in which they become separable.

The most popular kernel functions available are as follows:

- The linear kernel
- The polynomial kernel
- The RBF (Gaussian) kernel
- The string kernel

The linear kernel is often recommended for text classification, as most text classification problems need to be categorized into two classes. In our example, we also want to classify the SMS messages into spam and non-spam.

Solving the problem using linear SVM in Core ML

In this section, we are going to look at how we can solve the spam message detection problem using all the concepts we have gone through in this chapter.

We are going to take a bunch of SMS messages and attempt to classify them as spam or non-spam. This is a classification problem and we will use the linear SVM algorithm to perform this, considering the advantages of using this algorithm for text classification.

We are going to use NLP techniques to convert the data-SMS messages into a feature vector to feed into the linear SVM algorithm. We are going to use the scikit-learn vectorizer methods to transform the SMS messages into the TF-IDF vector, which could be fed into the linear SVM model to perform SMS spam detection (classification into spam and non-spam).

About the data

The data that we are using to create the model that detects the spam messages is taken from `http://www.dt.fee.unicamp.br/~tiago/smsspamcollection/`, which contains 747 spam message samples, along with 4,827 non-spam messages.

These messages are taken from different sources and labeled with the category of spam and non-spam. If you open the downloaded file in Notepad or any text editor, it will be in the following format:

```
ham    What you doing?how are you?
ham    Ok lar... Joking wif u oni...
 ham    dun say so early hor... U c already then say...
ham    MY NO. IN LUTON 0125698789 RING ME IF UR AROUND! H*
ham    Siva is in hostel aha:-.
ham    Cos i was out shopping with darren jus now n i called him 2 ask wat
present he wan lor. Then he started guessing who i was wif n he finally
guessed darren lor.
 spam   FreeMsg: Txt: CALL to No: 86888 & claim your reward of 3 hours talk
time to use from your phone now! ubscribe6GBP/ mnth inc 3hrs 16
stop?txtStop
 spam   Sunshine Quiz! Win a super Sony DVD recorder if you can name the
capital of Australia? Text MQUIZ to 82277. B
 spam   URGENT! Your Mobile No 07808726822 was awarded a L2,000 Bonus Caller
Prize on 02/09/03! This is our 2nd attempt to contact YOU! Call
0871-872-9758 BOX95QU
```

In the preceding sample, we can see that every line starts with the category name and is followed by the actual message.

Technical requirements

To create a model to classify a message as spam or non-spam, we need a library that is capable of doing so. Here, we've selected scikit-Learn.

To write this application, you need to have the Python3+ version installed on your desktop, and Xcode 9+ must be installed on your Mac machine. If you don't have either of these, please check the appendix of this book to learn how to get them. Once you have installed Python in your machine, execute the following commands to get the required packages:

```
pip install scikit-learn
pip install numpy
pip install coremltools
pip install pandas
```

Using the preceding code, we installed scikit-learn to get access to the algorithms and NumPy as the scikit-learn requires it, and pandas (*pandas* is an open source, BSD-licensed library providing high-performance, easy-to-use data structures and data analysis tools for the Python programming) to read the model from the file and core-ML tools to generate a Core ML model file.

Now, download `SMSSpamCollection.txt`, a plain text file from the model link stated in the preceding section, onto your disk and put it in your `project` folder.

Creating the Model file using Scikit Learn

In your project folder, create a python file with the following code to create a model file:

```
# importing required packages
import numpy as np
import pandas as pd

# Reading in and parsing data
raw_data = open('SMSSpamCollection.txt', 'r')
sms_data = []
for line in raw_data:
    split_line = line.split("\t")
    sms_data.append(split_line)

#Splitting data into messages and labels and training and test in y we are
```

```
having labels and x with the message text

sms_data = np.array(sms_data)
X = sms_data[:, 1]
y = sms_data[:, 0]

#Build a LinearSVC model
from sklearn.feature_extraction.text import TfidfVectorizer
from sklearn.svm import LinearSVC

#Build tf-idf vector representation of data
vectorizer = TfidfVectorizer()

# converting the message text as vector
vectorized_text = vectorizer.fit_transform(X)

text_clf = LinearSVC()
# fitting the model
text_clf = text_clf.fit(vectorized_text, y)
```

Test the fitted model, we can append the following code:

```
print text_clf.predict(vectorizer.transform(["""XXXMobileMovieClub: To use
your credit, click the WAP link in the next txt message or click here>>
http://wap. xxxmobilemovieclub.com?n=QJKGIGHJJGCBL"""]))
```

 Upon executing the preceding program, it will show you whether the
given message is spam or non-spam.

Converting the scikit-learn model into the Core ML model

In the preceding section, we created our model to classify the messages as spam and non-spam. Now, let's convert that into the Core ML model so that we can use that in an IOS app.

To create a core-ML model, append the following lines to the preceding code and run them. This will create a .mlmodel file:

```
# importing the library
import coremltools

# convert to fitted model in to coreml model
```

```
coreml_model = coremltools.converters.sklearn.convert(text_clf, "message",
"spam_or_not")

#set parameters of the model
coreml_model.short_description = "Classify whether message is spam or not"
coreml_model.input_description["message"] = "TFIDF of message to be
classified"
coreml_model.output_description["spam_or_not"] = "Whether message is spam
or not"

#save the model
coreml_model.save("SpamMessageClassifier.mlmodel")
```

Now, you can take the generated `SpamMessageClassifier.mlmodel` file and use this in your Xcode.

Writing the iOS application

You can get the code for the iOS project in our GitHub repository (`https://github.com/PacktPublishing/Machine-Learning-for-Mobile`). Once you download the project and open the project in Xcode, you will find the directory structure:

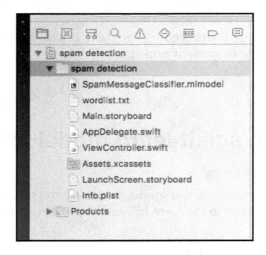

In this, I want to explain the important files to you. Main. Storyboard is having the UI design for the app:

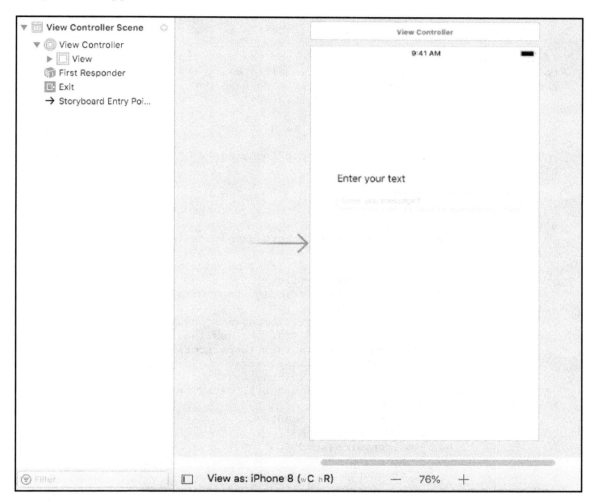

Here, we have two labels, one button, and one text box. The two labels are a heading label and on result label. Button to submit the input and get the result. And we have a textbox to give a message as input. Here, the main processing is written in the `controller.swift` view:

```
//common imports
import UIKit
import CoreML
```

```
class ViewController: UIViewController {
    //binding to the UI elements
    @IBOutlet weak var messageTextField: UITextField!
    @IBOutlet weak var messageLabel: UILabel!
    @IBOutlet weak var spamLabel: UILabel!

// This function will take the text from the user input and convert it in
to a vector format which our model requires using the wordslist.txt file
and the SMSSpamCollection.txt file that we have downloaded.
    func tfidf(sms: String) -> MLMultiArray{
        //get path for files
        let wordsFile = Bundle.main.path(forResource: "wordlist", ofType:
"txt")
        let smsFile = Bundle.main.path(forResource: "SMSSpamCollection",
ofType: "txt")
        do {
            //read words file
            let wordsFileText = try String(contentsOfFile: wordsFile!,
encoding: String.Encoding.utf8)
            var wordsData = wordsFileText.components(separatedBy:
.newlines)
            wordsData.removeLast() // Trailing newline.
            //read spam collection file
            let smsFileText = try String(contentsOfFile: smsFile!,
encoding: String.Encoding.utf8)
            var smsData = smsFileText.components(separatedBy: .newlines)
            smsData.removeLast() // Trailing newline.
            let wordsInMessage = sms.split(separator: " ")
            //create a multi-dimensional array
            let vectorized = try MLMultiArray(shape:
[NSNumber(integerLiteral: wordsData.count)], dataType:
MLMultiArrayDataType.double)
            for i in 0..<wordsData.count{
                let word = wordsData[i]
                if sms.contains(word){
                    var wordCount = 0
                    for substr in wordsInMessage{
                        if substr.elementsEqual(word){
                            wordCount += 1
                        }
                    }
                    let tf = Double(wordCount) /
Double(wordsInMessage.count)
                    var docCount = 0
                    for sms in smsData{
                        if sms.contains(word) {
                            docCount += 1
                        }
```

```
            }
            let idf = log(Double(smsData.count) / Double(docCount))
            vectorized[i] = NSNumber(value: tf * idf)
        } else {
            vectorized[i] = 0.0
        }
    }
    return vectorized
} catch {
    return MLMultiArray()
}
}
override func viewDidLoad() {
    super.viewDidLoad()
    // Do any additional setup after loading the view, typically from a
nib.
}
//This function will call when you click the predict button
@IBAction func predictSpam(_ sender: UIButton) {
    let enteredMessage =  messageTextField.text!
// checking and handling empty message.
    if (enteredMessage != ""){
        spamLabel.text = ""
    }
// Calling the preceding function to convert the text to vector
    let vec = tfidf(sms: enteredMessage)
    do {
// Passing input to the our model to get the prediction results.
        let prediction = try
SpamMessageClassifier().prediction(message: vec).spam_or_not
        print (prediction)
        if (prediction == "spam"){
            spamLabel.text = "SPAM!"
        }

// Our model is having ham as label for not spam messages so our model will
send the label as ham. Hence we are converting to Not Spam for displaying
purpose
        else if(prediction == "ham"){
            spamLabel.text = "NOT SPAM"
        }
    }
    catch{
            // catching the exception
        spamLabel.text = "No Prediction"
    }
}
}
```

When you run the app in the simulator of Xcode, it will generate the following results:

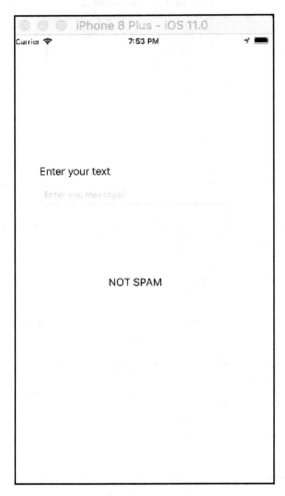

Summary

In this chapter, we went through many things, such as, understanding NLP at a high level. There are various steps involved in NLP, such as text preprocessing, as well as techniques to carry this out, such as feature engineering and methods to perform feature engineering and classification or clustering of the feature vectors. We also looked into the linear SVM algorithm in which we went through the details of the SVM algorithm, the kernel function, and how it is more applicable to text classification.

We solved our problem using linear SVM in Core ML and we also saw a practical example of performing spam message detection using the linear SVM algorithm model that we developed in scikit learn and converted into a Core ML model. We wrote an iOS application using the converted Core ML model.

In the next chapter, we will be introduced to another ML framework, Fritz, which tries to solve the common problems that we see in model deployment and upgrades, and the unification of handling ML models across mobile OS platforms.

8
Fritz

We have gone through mobile machine learning SDKs offered by Google—TensorFlow for mobile—and Apple—Core ML—in the previous chapters and got a good understanding of them. We looked at the basic architecture of those products, the key features they offer, and also tried a few tasks/programs using those SDKs. Based on what we have explored on the mobile machine learning frameworks and tools so far, we will be able to identify a few gaps that make it difficult to carry out mobile machine learning deployments and subsequent maintenance and support of those deployments. Let me list a few for you:

- Once we create the machine learning model and import it into the Android or iOS application, if there is any change that needs to be done to the model that was imported into the mobile application, how do you think this change will be implemented and upgraded to the application that is deployed and being used in the field? How is it possible to update/upgrade the model without redeploying the application in mobile application stores—the App Store or Play Store?

- Once the machine learning model is in the field and is being used by users in the field, how do we monitor the performance and usage of the model in real-time user scenarios?

- Also, you might have experienced that the process and mechanism to use the machine learning models in iOS and Android is not the same. Also, the mechanism to make the machine learning models created using a variety of machine learning frameworks, such as TensorFlow, and scikit-learn and, in order to make it compatible with TensorFlow Lite and Core ML is different. There is no common process and usage pattern that developers can follow to create and use these models across frameworks. We feel that if there was a common approach to use these machine learning models from different vendors using the same process and mechanism, it would be a lot more simple.

An attempt has been made by the Fritz platform to answer all the previously mentioned gaps observed in machine learning model usage and deployment. Fritz, as a machine learning platform, tries to provide solutions to facilitate machine learning model usage and deployment for mobile applications. It is a mobile machine learning platform with ready-to-use machine learning features, along with options to import and use custom ML models—TensorFlow for mobile and Core ML models.

So, in this chapter, we will be going through the following in detail:

- Understanding the Fritz mobile machine learning platform, its features, and its advantages.
- Exploring Fritz and implementing an iOS mobile application by using the regression model we already created using Core ML.
- Exploring Fritz and implementing an Android mobile application by using the sample Android model we created in `Chapter 3`, *Random Forest on iOS*, using TensorFlow for mobile.

Introduction to Fritz

Fritz is a free end-to-end platform that enables us to create machine learning-powered mobile applications easily. It is a platform that enables on-device machine learning, that is, it helps to create mobile machine learning applications that can completely work on mobile devices. It supports both iOS and Android platforms.

Prebuilt ML models

Fritz provides built-in ML models that can be directly used in mobile applications. Here are the two important models that Fritz supports:

- **Object detection**: You can identify objects of interest in an image or each frame of a live video. This helps you to know what objects are in an image, and where they are within the image. The object-detection feature makes predictions *completely on-device* and requires no internet connection.
- **Image labeling**: You can identify the contents of an image or each frame of live video. This also works completely offline and requires no internet connection.

Ability to use custom models

Fritz provides us with the ability to import models built for Core ML, TensorFlow for mobile, and TensorFlow Lite into mobile applications and provides APIs that can interact with these models directly.

Model management

The main advantage of Fritz is that it enables in ML model management and upgrades in real time:

- It provides us with the ability to upgrade the deployed machine learning models in the field, that is, it allows developers to upgrade or change the ML model without doing an application upgrade and redeploying in mobile application stores.
- It provides us with the facilities to monitor the performance of the machine learning models deployed into the field.
- It helps with deployment, analytics, and machine learning model management.

Hand-on samples using Fritz

In this section, we will try using Fritz and the models that we've already created for iOS and Android using Core ML and TensorFlow for mobile and build iOS and Android mobile applications using Fritz. Along with this, we will see how to use the Fritz built-in models, such as object detection and image labeling.

Using the existing TensorFlow for mobile model in an Android application using Fritz

In this section, we are going to see how to use a TensorFlow for mobile model that we already have created in an Android mobile application using the Fritz toolkit. We are going to take the sample model that we created using TensorFlow for mobile to do the summation $(a+b)$. We will go through the detailed steps required to achieve this objective.

Registering with Fritz

In order to use Fritz, you must sign up for an account at the Fritz web portal:

1. Go to `https://fritz.ai/`
2. Click on **Login** on the top menu
3. Click on **Create an account**
4. Enter your details and submit
5. Create a new project in Fritz

Once you have an account, log in using your credentials, and then perform the following steps:

1. Click on the **ADD A NEW PROJECT** button
2. Enter the project name and organization
3. Click on **Submit**

Uploading the model file (.pb or .tflite)

1. Click on **Custom Models** in the left-hand menu
2. Give the model name and a description
3. Upload the model file
4. Click on the **Create model file** button

Once it gets uploaded, the model page will look like this:

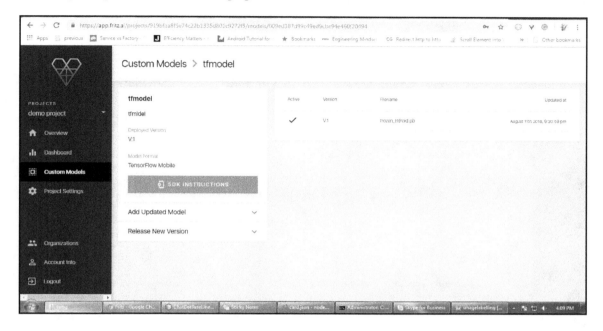

Here, we are using the same model that was created in `Chapter 3`, *Random Forest on iOS*: TensorFlow for Android. The GitHub URL is `https://github.com/PacktPublishing/Machine-Learning-for-Mobile/blob/master/tensorflow%20simple/tensor/frozen_tfdroid.pb`.

Setting up Android and registering the app

We have created a project and added a model to it. Let's see how to use this model in the Android project. Now, I am going to show you how to convert the TensorFlow simple example that we saw in `Chapter 3`, *Random Forest on iOS*, to the fritz format. To proceed, open that example in Android studio.

If you don't have it, you can download it from `https://github.com/PacktPublishing/Machine-Learning-for-Mobile/tree/master/tensorflow%20simple`. In the given path there TensorFlow sample is the Android project open it in the Android studio.

Adding Fritz's TFMobile library

In this section, we will convert this project into a Fritz-managed project. In the model page, click on the **SDK INSTRUCTIONS** button. It will open a dialog showing the integration information, as follows:

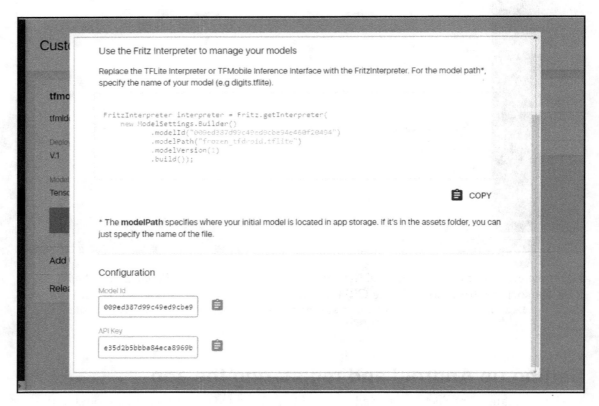

In this, you will find the **API Key**, which is unique for the project, the **Model Id**, which changes for every model that you have uploaded, and the code to create an interpreter.

Adding dependencies to the project

In order to access the Fritz interpreter, you need to add dependencies to your project. To do this, open the `build.gradle` file of your module app. You need to add a repository entry pointing to the Fritz Maven repository. To do this, add the following lines:

```
repositories {
    maven { url "https://raw.github.com/fritzlabs/fritz-repository/master"
}
}
```

Now add the Fritz dependencies:

```
dependencies {
    implementation fileTree(dir: 'libs', include: ['*.jar'])
    implementation 'com.android.support:appcompat-v7:27.1.0'
    implementation 'com.android.support.constraint:constraint-layout:1.1.2'
    implementation 'ai.fritz:core:1.0.0'
    implementation 'ai.fritz:custom-model-tfmobile:1.0.0'
    implementation 'com.stripe:stripe-android:6.1.2'
}
```

With the preceding code, we have added the Fritz core libraries and the `tfmobile` library. The Fritz core libraries are required to communicate with the fritz cloud server to download the model files for version management. The `tfmobile` libraries are required as we are using the TensorFlow mobile model and we need the TensorFlow libraries for the inference.

Registering the FritzJob service in your Android Manifest

I already mentioned that your app will download the model files when deployed in the fritz cloud server. To do that, Fritz has implemented a service, named `FritzJob` service, which will be running in the background. When it finds a new model deployed in your web console, it will try to download it when the device is connected to the Wi-Fi.

To log into your cloud account, your app requires some credentials. For that, fritz supplies an API key. To enable this, we need to add a meta entry in your Android manifest XML file, as follows:

```
<meta-data android:name="fritz_api_key"
android:value="6265ed5e7e334a97bbc750a09305cb19" />
```

The value of the fritz API key you need to replace with yours that you got from the previous dialog in the browser when you clicked **SDK INSTRUCTIONS**.

And we need to declare the Fritz job, as follows:

```
<service
    android:name="ai.fritz.core.FritzJob"
    android:exported="true"
    android:permission="android.permission.BIND_JOB_SERVICE" />
```

As our app needs to connect to a cloud server through Wi-Fi, we need to mention the internet access permission for that:

```
<uses-permission android:name="android.permission.INTERNET"/>
```

Now, my whole manifest file will look like this:

```
<?xml version="1.0" encoding="utf-8"?>
<manifest xmlns:android="http://schemas.android.com/apk/res/android"
    package="org.packt.fritz.samplefritzapp">

    <uses-permission android:name="android.permission.INTERNET"/>

    <application
        android:allowBackup="true"
        android:icon="@mipmap/ic_launcher"
        android:label="@string/app_name"
        android:roundIcon="@mipmap/ic_launcher_round"
        android:supportsRtl="true"
        android:theme="@style/AppTheme">
        <activity android:name=".MainActivity">
            <intent-filter>
                <action android:name="android.intent.action.MAIN" />

                <category android:name="android.intent.category.LAUNCHER" />
            </intent-filter>
        </activity>
        <meta-data android:name="fritz_api_key"
android:value="6265ed5e7e334a97bbc750a09305cb19" />
        <service
            android:name="ai.fritz.core.FritzJob"
            android:exported="true"
            android:permission="android.permission.BIND_JOB_SERVICE" />
    </application>

</manifest>
```

Replacing the TensorFlowInferenceInterface class with Fritz Interpreter

Open the main activity of your app and make the following changes:

```
package org.packt.fritz.samplefritzapp;

import android.os.Bundle;
import android.support.v7.app.AppCompatActivity;
import android.view.View;
import android.widget.Button;
import android.widget.EditText;
import android.widget.TextView;
import android.widget.Toast;

import org.tensorflow.contrib.android.TensorFlowInferenceInterface;

import ai.fritz.core.*;
import ai.fritz.customtfmobile.*;
```

In the preceding `import` statements, we have added imports for the Fritz core library and Fritz custom model library, and we are also using the Google `TensorflowInfereceInterface`:

```
public class MainActivity extends AppCompatActivity {

private TensorFlowInferenceInterface inferenceInterface;

  static {
System.loadLibrary("tensorflow_inference");
  }
```

In the preceding lines, we have declared the TensorFlow inference interface and loaded the `tensorflow_inference` library, which is optional. This can be implicitly done by Fritz itself:

```
@Override
protected void onCreate(Bundle savedInstanceState) {
        super.onCreate(savedInstanceState);
setContentView(R.layout.activity_main);
Fritz.configure(this);
```

In the preceding lines, we have configured the fritz service and linked it with the app. Here, it will verify whether the app package name is added to your Fritz console.

To do so, you need to click **Project Settings** in the left-hand menu of your project in the Fritz web console.

Then, click on **Add android app** to your project and it will open a dialog, as follows:

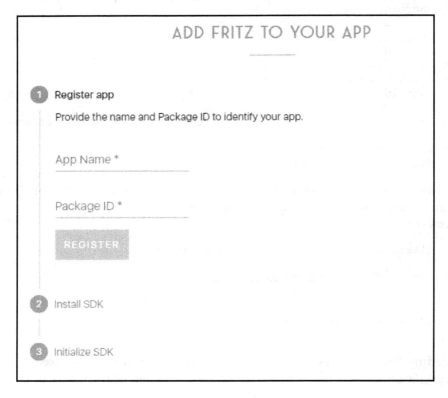

In this, you need to give a name to your app, for identification purposes. And then you need to get the package name from your Android manifest file and enter it in the **Package ID** text field.

This particular one you can get from the manifest tag of your manifest file, as follows:

```
<?xml version="1.0" encoding="utf-8"?>
<manifest xmlns:android="http://schemas.android.com/apk/res/android"
    package="org.packt.fritz.samplefritzapp">
```

Once you register that, come back to our code:

```
try {

FritzTFMobileInterpreter interpreter =
FritzTFMobileInterpreter.create(this.getApplicationContext(),
 new ModelSettings.Builder()
.modelId("2a83207a32334fceaa29498f57cbd9ae")
.modelPath("ab2.pb")
.modelVersion(1)
.build());
```

Here, we are creating an object for our Fritz model. The first argument is the application context object, and the second argument is the model information object.

In the model settings, we will provide the model ID, This can be obtained from the dialog shown when you click the SDK instructions in your model page of the Fritz web console.

The other important thing is the model path. This is your model file name, which you placed in the assets folder:

```
inferenceInterface = interpreter.getInferenceInterface();
```

In the preceding line, we are getting the TensorFlow inference interface object and assigning it to the globally declared variable:

```
final Button button = (Button) findViewById(R.id.button);

button.setOnClickListener(new View.OnClickListener() {
public void onClick(View v) {

final EditText editNum1 = (EditText) findViewById(R.id.editNum1);
final EditText editNum2 = (EditText) findViewById(R.id.editNum2);


float num1 = Float.parseFloat(editNum1.getText().toString());
float num2 = Float.parseFloat(editNum2.getText().toString());

long[] i = {1};

int[] a = {Math.round(num1)};
int[] b = {Math.round(num2)};

inferenceInterface.feed("a", a, i);
inferenceInterface.feed("b", b, i);

inferenceInterface.run(new String[]{"c"});

int[] c = {0};
inferenceInterface.fetch("c", c);

final TextView textViewR = (TextView) findViewById(R.id.txtViewResult);
textViewR.setText(Integer.toString(c[0]));
 }
});
 }
 catch (Exception ex)
{
Toast.makeText(this.getApplicationContext(),ex.toString(),Toast.LENGTH_LONG
).show();

 }


 }


 }
```

In the preceding block, we have registered an event listener, which will perform the inference whenever a user clicks the **Run** button.

Building and running the application

To view the result, connect a device and run the project. It will show the result, as follows:

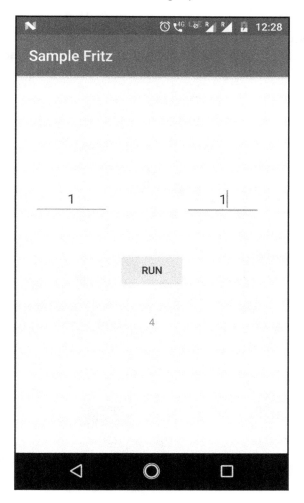

Deploying a new version of your model

The real power of Fritz exists in the automatic download of revised model files. Here, we will demonstrate this.

So far, we have uploaded our old $(a+b)^2$ model and performed the inference. Now, we will update it to $(a+b)^3$ and check whether our app automatically downloads the revised model.

For that, we need to create the $(a+b)^3$ model. First, we need to recall our *Creating and saving model* section under Chapter 4, *TensorFlow Mobile in Android*, where we created the $(a+b)^2$ model. We are going to make a small change that will convert this model:

```
import tensorflow as tf

a = tf.placeholder(tf.int32, name='a')  # input
b = tf.placeholder(tf.int32, name='b')  # input
times = tf.Variable(name="times", dtype=tf.int32, initial_value=3)
c = tf.pow(tf.add(a, b), times, name="c")

saver = tf.train.Saver()
init_op = tf.global_variables_initializer()
with tf.Session() as sess:
    sess.run(init_op)

    tf.train.write_graph(sess.graph_def, '.', 'tfdroid.pbtxt')
    sess.run(tf.assign(name="times", value=3, ref=times))
    # save the graph

    # save a checkpoint file, which will store the above assignment
    saver.save(sess, './tfdroid.ckpt')
```

 In the preceding program, the only change we have made is to the value of the `times` variable, which is now 3. This will result in multiplying (a+b) by three, which gives $(a+b)^3$. Please refer to Chapter 4, *TensorFlow Mobile in Android*, for instructions on how to run and generate the .pb extension model file.

Once you get the `frozen_tfdroid.pb` file, you can upload this from the Fritz web console of your model page, as shown in the following screenshot:

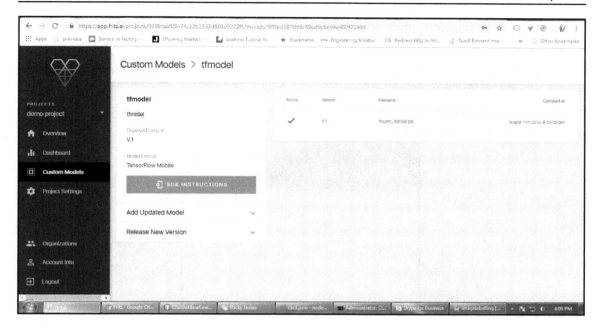

Expand the **Add Updated Model** pane and upload the generated model. It will add as version 2 in the right-hand side table:

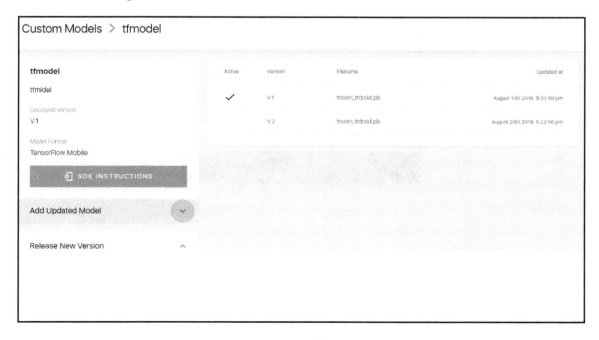

Now you have uploaded a revision of the model, but you haven't published it yet. To do so, you need to expand the **Release New Version** pane and release the version you need.

Once you do that, all the mobile devices that installed your app will download the released model when they get an internet connection through a WiFi network.

Here is the result I got when I connected to my WiFi router and restarted the app:

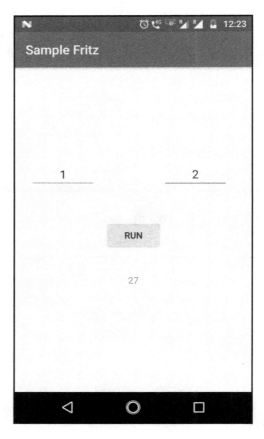

Creating an android application using fritz pre-built models

Fritz offers two pre-built models for both iOS and Android:

- Image labeling
- Object detection

In this section, we are going to see how to use the image-labeling model in your Android app.

To do this, you need to create a project in Fritz; please refer to the steps given in the *Using existing TensorFlow for mobile model in Android application using Fritz* section.

Now, open Android studio and create an empty project with empty activity and layout files.

Adding dependencies to the project

In order to access the fritz interpreter shown in the preceding dialog, you need to add dependencies to your project. To do this, open the `build.gradle` file of your module app.

You need to add a repository entry pointing to the fritz maven repository. To do that, add the following lines:

```
repositories {
    maven { url "https://raw.github.com/fritzlabs/fritz-repository/master"
}
}
```

Now, add the fritz dependencies:

```
dependencies {
    implementation fileTree(dir: 'libs', include: ['*.jar'])
    implementation 'com.android.support:appcompat-v7:26.1.0'
    implementation 'com.android.support.constraint:constraint-layout:1.1.2'
    implementation 'ai.fritz:core:1.0.1'
    implementation 'ai.fritz:vision-label-model:1.0.1'

}
```

With the preceding lines, we have added the fritz core libraries and fritz vision library for labeling. Fritz core libraries are required to communicate with the fritz cloud server in order to download the model files for version management.

The Fritz vision library for labeling will download the required libraries, such as TensorFlow mobile and vision dependencies.

Registering the Fritz JobService in your Android Manifest

I already mentioned that your app will download the model files when deployed in the fritz cloud server. To do that, Fritz has implemented a service named `FritzJob`. This service will be running in the background and when it finds a new model deployed in your web console, it will try to download it when the device is connected through the WiFi network.

To log into your cloud account, your app requires some credentials. For that, fritz is supplying an API key. To enable this, we need to add a meta-entry to your Android manifest XML file, as follows:

```
<meta-data
    android:name="fritz_api_key"
    android:value="e35d2b5bbba84eca8969b7d6acac1fb7" />
```

The value of the Fritz API key you need to replace with yours that you got from the previous dialog in the browser when you clicked SDK INSTRUCTIONS.

We need to declare the Fritz job, as follows:

```
<service
    android:name="ai.fritz.core.FritzJob"
    android:exported="true"
    android:permission="android.permission.BIND_JOB_SERVICE" />
```

As our app needs to connect to a cloud server through WiFi, we need to mention the internet access permission for that:

```
<uses-permission android:name="android.permission.INTERNET"/>
```

And we need to add the following lines:

```
<uses-sdk android:minSdkVersion="21" android:targetSdkVersion="21" />
<uses-feature android:name="android.hardware.camera2.full" />
<uses-permission android:name="android.permission.CAMERA" />
```

In Android, the camera handling mechanism has been changed to the `camera2` package, and the preceding line specifies which `camera2` feature to use. To learn more about this, check out https://developer.android.com/reference/android/hardware/camera2/ CameraCharacteristics#INFO_SUPPORTED_HARDWARE_LEVEL. So, to access the camera, we are adding camera permission also.

Now, my whole manifest file will look like this:

```xml
<?xml version="1.0" encoding="utf-8"?>
<manifest xmlns:android="http://schemas.android.com/apk/res/android"
    package="com.example.avinaas.imagelabelling">

    <uses-sdk android:minSdkVersion="21" android:targetSdkVersion="21" />
    <uses-feature android:name="android.hardware.camera2.full" />
    <uses-permission android:name="android.permission.CAMERA" />
    <uses-permission android:name="android.permission.INTERNET" />

    <application
        android:allowBackup="true"
        android:icon="@mipmap/ic_launcher"
        android:label="@string/app_name"
        android:roundIcon="@mipmap/ic_launcher_round"
        android:supportsRtl="true"
        android:theme="@style/AppTheme">
        <activity android:name=".MainActivity">
            <intent-filter>
                <action android:name="android.intent.action.MAIN" />

                <category android:name="android.intent.category.LAUNCHER"
/>
            </intent-filter>
        </activity>
        <meta-data
            android:name="fritz_api_key"
            android:value="e35d2b5bbba84eca8969b7d6acac1fb7" />
        <service
            android:name="ai.fritz.core.FritzJob"
            android:exported="true"
            android:permission="android.permission.BIND_JOB_SERVICE" />
    </application>

</manifest>
```

Creating the app layout and components

In your `activity_main.xml` file, which resides in your `assets/layouts` folder, you need to input the following code:

```xml
<?xml version="1.0" encoding="utf-8"?>
<RelativeLayout xmlns:android="http://schemas.android.com/apk/res/android"
    xmlns:tools="http://schemas.android.com/tools"
    android:layout_width="match_parent"
    android:layout_height="match_parent"
    tools:context="com.example.avinaas.imagelabelling.MainActivity">

<TextureView
    android:id="@+id/preview"
    android:layout_width="match_parent"
    android:layout_height="wrap_content"
    android:layout_above="@id/btn_takepic"
    android:layout_alignParentTop="true"/>

    <Button
        android:id="@+id/btn_takepic"
        android:layout_width="wrap_content"
        android:layout_height="wrap_content"
        android:layout_alignParentBottom="true"
        android:layout_centerHorizontal="true"
        android:layout_marginBottom="16dp"
        android:layout_marginTop="16dp"
        android:text="Start Labeling"
        />
</RelativeLayout>
```

 In the preceding XML tools, the context value needs to change with your main activity.

In the preceding XML, we have added a button to receive events, and a texture view, which serves as a placeholder for the camera stream.

The design view of the preceding layout will look like this:

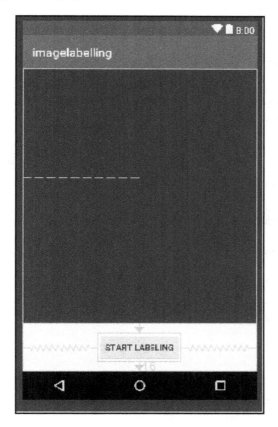

Coding the application

The code for this application can be found in your GitHub repository at https://github.
com/PacktPublishing/Machine-Learning-for-Mobile/tree/master/Fritz/
imagelabelling/imagelabelling.

Once you have downloaded the code open it in Android studio here you can find the code
in the MainActivity.java.

To explain the whole code, it may deal more with android code. Here, you can find the explanation of the important code blocks:

```
Fritz.configure(this.getApplicationContext());
```

The preceding line in the `oncreate` life cycle method will initialize the Fritz framework:

```
options = new FritzVisionLabelPredictorOptions.Builder()
        .confidenceThreshold(0.3f)
        .build();
```

The preceding line will create the configuration options for the label predictor:

```
visionPredictor =
FritzVisionLabelPredictor.getInstance(this.getApplicationContext(),
options);
```

Creating the instance of the predictor:

```
Bitmap bmp = BitmapFactory.decodeFile(file.getPath());
```

Getting the image saved to the file and converting this as a bitmap:

```
FritzVisionImage img = FritzVisionImage.fromBitmap(bmp);
List<FritzVisionLabel> labels = visionPredictor.predict(img);
```

Converting the bitmap image to fritz vision image and supplying that image object to the predictor's `predit` method, which, in turn, returns the predicted labels as the list:

```
String output="";

for(FritzVisionLabel lab: labels)
{
    output = output + lab.getText()+"\t Confidence: "+ lab.getConfidence();
}

if(output.trim().length()==0)
{
    output = "Unable to predict.";
}
Toast.makeText(MainActivity.this, output, Toast.LENGTH_LONG).show();
```

As the predictor returned a list of `Fritzvisionlabel` objects, we need to decode that and show it to the user. The preceding code shows the content and the confidence percentage to the user in a Toast message.

Once you run the app, the image frames captured from the camera will be shown in the texture view that we have created in our layout.

Once you click the **start labelling** button, it will save the image to the disk and input the same image to the `Fritzvisionlabel` predictor. Once you revive the prediction results, you will be interpreting it and showing it to the user in the form of a `Toast` message.

To make the preceding app work, we need to add this app to your Fritz project.

To do so, click **Project Settings** in the left-hand menu of your project in the Fritz web console.

Then, click on **Add android app to your project** and it will open a dialog, as follows:

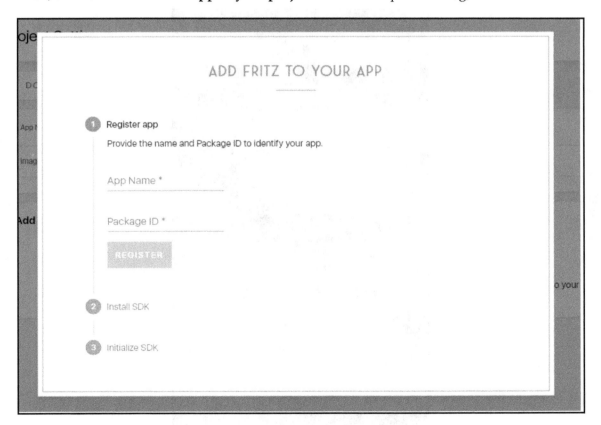

In this, you need to give a name to your app, for identification purposes. Then you need to get the package name from your android manifest file and enter it in the `Package ID` text field.

This can be obtained from the manifest tag of your manifest file as follows:

```xml
<?xml version="1.0" encoding="utf-8"?>
<manifest xmlns:android="http://schemas.android.com/apk/res/android"
    package="com.example.avinaas.imagelabelling">
```

Once you register the app, you can run and see the result by connecting an Android device to your PC with the USB-debugging option enabled.

Make sure you disable the **Instant run** option in your android studio. This can be done from the settings option in the file menu.

Once you successfully run the app, the results will look like this:

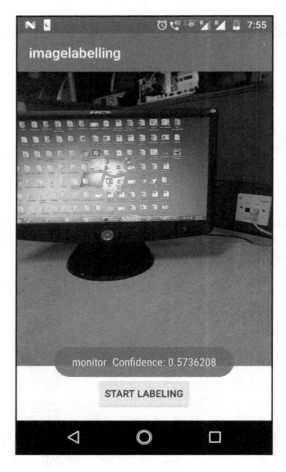

Using the existing Core ML model in an iOS application using Fritz

In this section, we are going to see how to use a Core ML model that we already have created in an iOS mobile application using the Fritz toolkit. We are going to take the `HousePricer.mlmodel` that we created using Core ML using the `Boston` dataset and perform house price prediction using a linear regression algorithm. We will detail the steps required to achieve this objective.

For this, please download the source code of the linear regression example in pack GitHub for house price prediction at `https://github.com/PacktPublishing/Machine-Learning-for-Mobile/tree/master/housing%20price%20prediction/sample`.

Registering with Fritz

In order to use fritz, you must sign up for an account in the fritz web portal:

1. Go to `https://fritz.ai/`.
2. Click on **Login** on the top menu
3. Click on **Create an account**
4. Enter your details and submit

Creating a new project in Fritz

Once you have an account, log in using your credentials and perform the following steps:

1. Click on the **Add new project** button
2. Enter the project name and organization
3. Click on **Submit**

Uploading the model file (.pb or .tflite)

The following are the steps to upload the model file:

1. Click on **Custom Models** in the left-hand menu
2. Give the model name and a description
3. Upload the model file (`HousePricer.mlmodel`) that got generated in the first linear regression chapter after you ran the Python program

 You can find this file in the downloaded directory: `https://github.com/ PacktPublishing/Machine-Learning-for-Mobile/tree/master/ housing%20price%20prediction/sample/sample`.

4. Click on the **Create model file** button

Once it gets uploaded, the model page will look like this:

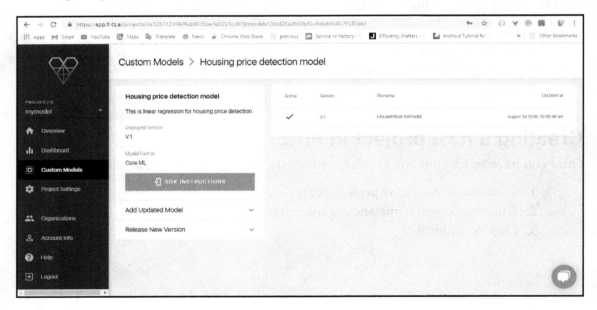

Creating an Xcode project

Now, open the project that you have downloaded in Xcode. The project will look like this.

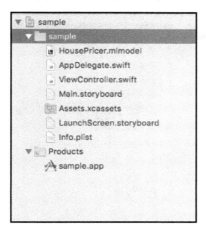

Installing Fritz dependencies

To install Fritz dependencies, download the pod file for your model from Fritz. For that, you need to add your iOS project to your fritz project. This you can do from the project settings page in the fritz console.

In the project settings page, click on the **Add an IOS project** button. Then fill in the dialog with the app name shown in the Xcode when you open your app. Fill this in with the bundle ID that you can get from the build settings, as shown in the following screenshot:

You will then be allowed to download the `Fritz-info.plist` file. Add this file to your project folder in Xcode, as shown in the following screenshot:

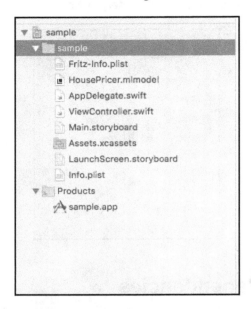

After that, you need to close Xcode, navigate to your project folder from a terminal, and give the following commands, one by one:

```
$ pod init
$ pod 'Fritz'
$ pod install
```

This creates a `.xcworkspace` file for your app. Use this file for all future developments on your application.

Now close your Xcode application and re-open the project using this file.

Adding code

Open your model console in the fritz console. It will have a button - SDK Instructions click on this it will open a dialog as shown in the following screenshot. As shown in the dialog box, create a new file with the filename shown and paste/write the code in it:

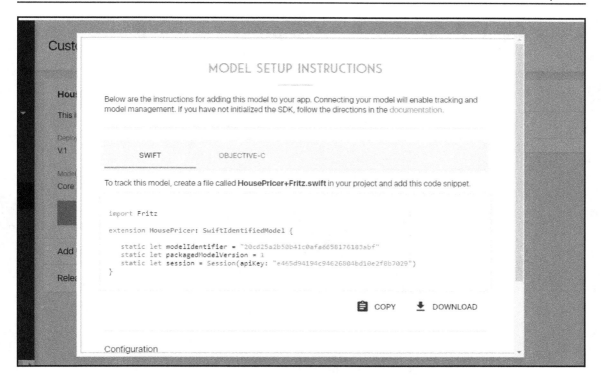

Now, once you have added this file, you need to open `AppDelegate.swift` and make the following modifications:

- First, add a new import as
- Import `Fritz`
- Now in app delegate class:

```
func application(_application : UIApplication,
didFinishLaunchingWithOptions launchOptions:
[UIApplication.LauncgOptionsKey: Any])
```

Replace the previously method definition as shown here:

```
func application(_ application: UIApplication,
didFinishLaunchingWithOptions launchOptions:
[UIApplication.LaunchOptionsKey: Any]?)
-> Bool {
FritzCore.configure()
return true
}
```

Building and running the iOS mobile application

Similar to how we build the iOS mobile applications, build and run the project in an emulator and it will give you the following results:

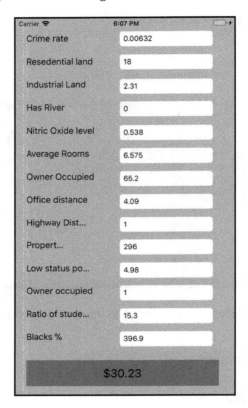

Summary

In this chapter, we learned about Fritz, an end-to-end platform that enables us to create machine learning applications. We also looked at pre-built ML models and how to use custom models in Fritz. Then, we explored how we can implement Fritz in Core ML in iOS and Android. Finally, we created two applications using the Fritz library: one using a pre-built fritz model, and the other using a Core ML model for iOS. In the next chapter, we will learn about neural networks and their uses for mobile applications and machine learning.

Neural Networks on Mobile

9

In `Chapter 2`, *Supervised and Unsupervised Learning Algorithms*, when we introduced you to TensorFlow, its components, and how it works, we talked briefly about **convolutional neural networks** (**CNNs**) and how they work. In this chapter, we will delve into the basic concepts of neural networks. We will explore the similarities and variations between machine learning and neural networks.

We will also go through some of the challenges of executing deep learning algorithms on mobile devices. We will briefly go through the various deep learning and neural network SDKs available for mobile applications that can be run on mobile devices directly. Toward the end of this chapter, we will create an interesting assignment that will utilize both TensorFlow and Core ML.

In this chapter, we will be cover the following topics:

- Creating a TensorFlow image recognition model
- Converting the TensorFlow model into a Core ML model
- Creating an iOS mobile application that utilizes the Core ML model
- Introduction to Keras
- Creating a handwritten digit recognition solution

In this chapter, we are going to implement all of the major topics we have gone through in this book. Before proceeding, make sure you have gone through all the previous chapters in this book.

Introduction to neural networks

A neural network is a system of hardware and/or software that is modeled on the operation of neurons in the human brain. The design behind neural networks is inspired by the human brain and its functionality. Let's understand the design of the human brain. The neuron is the basic working unit of the brain. It's a specialized cell that can transmit information to other nerve cells. The brain is made up of approximately 100,000,000,000 neurons. A neuron's main function is to process and transmit information.

Communication steps of a neuron

Neuron communication follows a four-step path:

- A neuron receives information from the external environment or from other neurons.
- The neuron integrates, or processes, the information from all of its input and determines whether to send an output signal. This integration takes place both in time (the duration of the input and the time between input) and space (across the surface of the neuron).
- The neuron propagates the signal along its length at a high speed.
- The neuron converts this electrical signal to a chemical one and transmits it to another neuron or to an effect such as a muscle or gland.

 To get a better understanding of how neurons—the basic building blocks of the human brain—work, check out `http://www.biologyreference.com/Mo-Nu/Neuron.html#ixzz5ZD78t97u`.

Now, coming to the neurons' artificial neural networks, the function of these neurons is to take in some input and fire an output.

The activation function

To express this categorically, the neuron is a placeholder function that takes in inputs, processes them by applying the function on the input, and produces the output. Any simple function can be put in the defined placeholder:

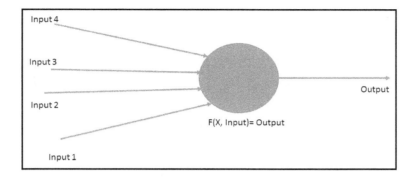

The function that's used in a neuron is generally called an activation function. In the human body, there are three types of neurons: sensory neurons, motor neurons, and interneurons. In the artificial world, the activation function would probably create the different capability and functionality of the neuron.

Here are a few commonly used activation functions:

- step
- sigmoid
- tanh
- ReLU-Rectified
- Linear Unit (used mostly in deep learning)

It is outside the scope of this book to delve into the details of each function. However, it will be good for you to understand these functions and their intricacies if you want to study neural networks further.

Arrangement of neurons

Let's look at the arrangement of neurons in the human body. A typical neuron has several dendrites, normally arranged in an extremely branched fashion, in order to establish contact with many other neurons. Neurons in the human body are also arranged in layers. The number of these layers varies across different parts of the body and brain, but normally is ranges from three to six layers.

In the artificial world, these neurons are also arranged as layers. The following diagram will help you understand the organization of neurons:

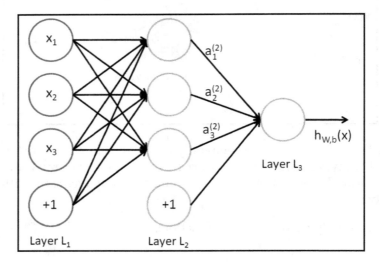

The leftmost layer of the network is called the **input layer**, and the rightmost layer is called the **output layer**. The middle layer of neurons is called the **hidden layer** because its values are not observed in the training set.

In this sample neural network, there are three inputs, three hidden units, and one output unit. Any neural network will have at least one input and one output layer. The number of hidden layers can vary.

The activation function used in each hidden layer can be different for the same network. This means that the activation function for hidden layer 1 and the b activation function for hidden layer 2 of the same network.

Types of neural networks

Neural networks vary based on the number of hidden layers and the activation functions used in each layer. Here are some of the common types of neural networks:

- **Deep neural networks**: Networks with more than one hidden layer.

- **CNN**: Commonly used in computer-vision-related learning problems. The CNN hidden layer uses convolution functions as the activation function.
- **Recurrent neural networks**: Commonly used in problems related to natural language processing.

Current projects/research in the field of improving neural networks in mobile devices include the following:

- MobileNet
- MobileNet V2
- MNasNet—implementing reinforcement learning in mobile devices

Image recognition solution

Imagine you go to a restaurant with your friends. Assume you are a fitness freak and though you have come to the party to enjoy the buffet, as a fitness freak, you are calorie conscious and don't want to go overboard.

Now, imagine you have a mobile application that comes to your rescue: it takes a picture of the dish, identifies its ingredients, and calculates the caloric value of the food! You could take a picture of every dish and calculate its caloric value and can then decide whether to put it on your plate. Further, this app keeps on learning the different dishes that you take pictures of and continues to learn and master itself in this trade so that it can take very good care of your health.

I can see the sparkle in your eyes. Yes, this is the mobile application we want to try in this chapter. We also want to utilize both TensorFlow and Core ML to accomplish this activity. We will be performing the following steps to create the application that we just discussed:

1. Create the TensorFlow image recognition model
2. Convert it into a .ml model file
3. Create an iOS/SWIFT app to use that model

We will go through each of these steps in detail in the upcoming sections.

Creating a TensorFlow image recognition model

TensorFlow is an open source software library for data flow programming across a range of tasks. It is a symbolic math library and is also used for machine learning applications, such as neural networks. It is used for both research and production at Google, often replacing its closed source predecessor, DistBelief. TensorFlow was developed by the Google Brain team for internal Google use. It was released under the Apache 2.0 open source license on November 9, 2015.

TensorFlow is cross-platform. It runs on nearly everything: GPUs and CPUs–including mobile and embedded platforms–and even **tensor processing units** (**TPUs**), which are specialized hardware for performing tensor math.

What does TensorFlow do?

To keep it simple, let's assume you want two numbers. Now, if you want to write a program in a regular programming language, such as Python, you would use the following:

$$a = 1$$

$$b = 2$$

$$print(a+b)$$

If you run the program, you will see the output as 3, and then you'll see the same implementation on `tensorflow`:

```
import tensorflow as tf
x = tf.constant(35, name='x')
y = tf.Variable(x + 5, name='y')
model = tf.global_variables_initializer()
with tf.Session() as session:
    session.run(model)
    print(session.run(y))
```

Let me explain the preceding code. First, we are creating a constant with node name x, adding 5 to it, and storing it in another variable/node y. If you can see the output of the console of y at this point, you will find the definition of the node, but not the value of 40.

Here, you are defining the nodes of the graph and its corresponding operations. You can make use of the graph once you initialize the variables and create and get a session/instance of the graph.

The following diagram will help you understand this concept:

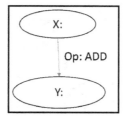

In TensorFlow, all of the constants, placeholders, and variables we will use to create the definition and the linkage between nodes will create one graph, which is just like your class concept in object-oriented programming. Think of the graph as a class and the nodes as data members, `tf.globalvariableinitilizer()` as calling the static method to initialize the constants and variable, and `session.run()` as calling the constructor of a class.

Retraining the model

To create an image classifier, we need to go through many things and do a lot of coding. To keep it simple, we will be showing you how to create it using the Google Code Lab provided code. The following content was taken from Google's Code Lab tutorial.

This was made using CNNs. Explaining all of this is outside the scope of this book. We briefly explored CNN in the introduction of this chapter. However that is very less, compared to what is an ocean. For more information, interested readers can check out https://colah.github.io/posts/2014-07-Conv-Nets-Modular/.

Let's see how easily we can create an image classifier in `tensorflow`. To get started, we need to install anaconda and then run the following commands:

```
conda create -n tensorflow pip python=3.6
```

Once you run the preceding command, you will get the following prompt:

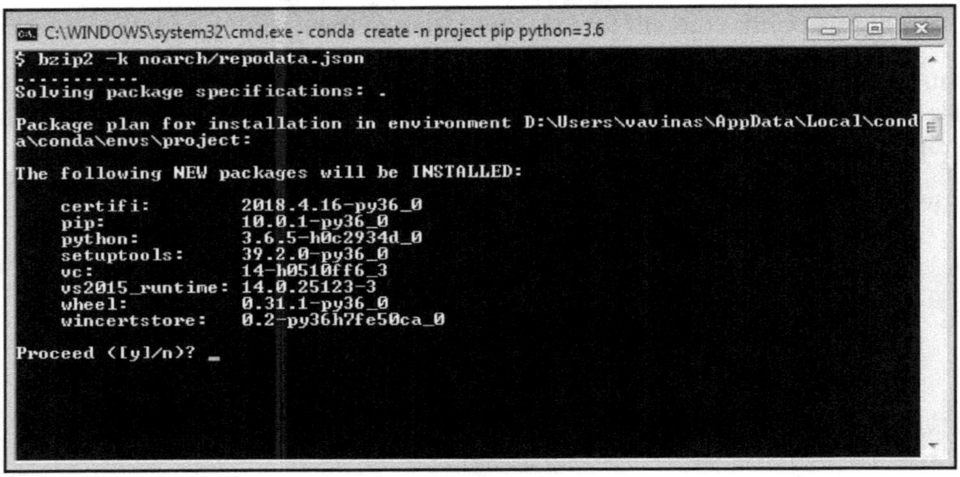

Type y to proceed. Once the command has successfully executed, you will see the following screen:

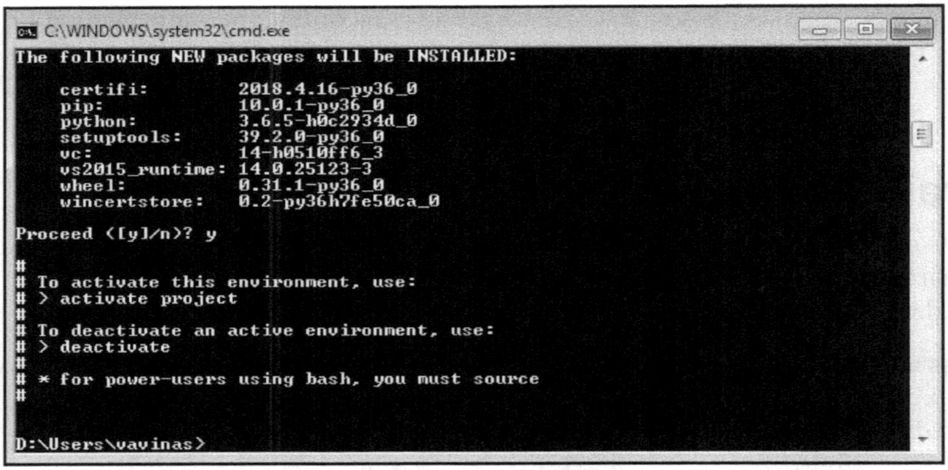

Type activate project. Once the project has been activated, you will see the prompt, like so:

```
(project) D:\Users\vavinas>
```

Then, type the following commands:

```
pip install tensorflow
```

Use the following command to verify the installed packages:

```
pip list
```

It has to produce the following result. If you don't see some of these packages in your machine, reinstall them:

Now, we have successfully installed `tensorflow` and its dependencies. Let's get the code from Google Code Labs that will do the classification. For this, make sure you have installed Git on your machine. There are several ways to install it, but the simplest way is through npm.

To check that Git is properly installed, type `git` in the opened command prompt. You will see all the options available for that command. If it is prompting as `invalid command`, please try to install it correctly. Now, let's execute the command to clone the repository:

```
git clone https://github.com/googlecodelabs/tensorflow-for-poets-2
```

Once you are done, go to `tensorflow-for-poets-2` using the following command:

```
cd tensorflow-for-poets-2
```

The following folder contains all of the that are scripts required to train a model for image recognition. If you check the `tf_file` folder, it will be empty. Here, we will be using this folder to keep the training images and train the model using the scripts in the scripts folder.

To input the images, you need to first download the images. For our sample, we are using food images with four class labels. You can download it from our Git repository, `project/food_photos`, and then paste that folder into `tf_files`. If you are unable to execute this command, open the folder in Internet Explorer, and then download the in `tensorflow-for-poets-2/tf_files` file.

Extract the files into flat files, as shown here:

Now, we are going to retrain the model using the following script. Execute the following command:

```
python -m scripts.retrain \
  --bottleneck_dir=tf_files/bottlenecks \
  --how_many_training_steps=500 \
  --model_dir=tf_files/models/ \
  --summaries_dir=tf_files/training_summaries/ mobilenet_0.50_224 \
  --output_graph=tf_files/retrained_graph.pb \
  --output_labels=tf_files/retrained_labels.txt \
  --architecture=mobilenet_0.50_224 \
  --image_dir=tf_files/food_photos
```

The previous Python script is used to retrain a model that has many arguments, but we will use and discuss only a few important arguments, as follows:

- `bottleneck_dir`: This will save these files to the bottlenecks/ directory.
- `how_many_training_steps`: This will a number below 4,000. A higher number will give your model greater accuracy, but takes too much time to build, and the model file will be too big.

- `model_dir`: This tells us where to save the model.
- `summaries_dir`: Contains the training summaries.
- `output_graph`: Where to save the output graph. This is the resultant model that we will use in mobiles.
- `output_labels`: This is the file that holds the class labels. Usually, the class label for an image is the folder name.
- `architecture`: This tells us which architecture to use. Here, we are using the mobilenet model with a 0.50 relative size of the model and a 244 image size.
- `image_dir`: Inputs the images directory, in this case, `food_photos`.

Executing the previous command will give you the following as output:

```
C:\WINDOWS\system32\cmd.exe
INFO:tensorflow:2018-06-21 12:10:48.218886: Step 460: Cross entropy = 0.105809
INFO:tensorflow:2018-06-21 12:10:48.307895: Step 460: Validation accuracy = 88.0
% (N=100)
INFO:tensorflow:2018-06-21 12:10:49.255990: Step 470: Train accuracy = 98.0%
INFO:tensorflow:2018-06-21 12:10:49.255990: Step 470: Cross entropy = 0.159459
INFO:tensorflow:2018-06-21 12:10:49.336998: Step 470: Validation accuracy = 90.0
% (N=100)
INFO:tensorflow:2018-06-21 12:10:50.286093: Step 480: Train accuracy = 100.0%
INFO:tensorflow:2018-06-21 12:10:50.286093: Step 480: Cross entropy = 0.058190
INFO:tensorflow:2018-06-21 12:10:50.394104: Step 480: Validation accuracy = 91.0
% (N=100)
INFO:tensorflow:2018-06-21 12:10:51.371202: Step 490: Train accuracy = 99.0%
INFO:tensorflow:2018-06-21 12:10:51.371202: Step 490: Cross entropy = 0.081113
INFO:tensorflow:2018-06-21 12:10:51.477212: Step 490: Validation accuracy = 87.0
% (N=100)
INFO:tensorflow:2018-06-21 12:10:52.359300: Step 499: Train accuracy = 97.0%
INFO:tensorflow:2018-06-21 12:10:52.359300: Step 499: Cross entropy = 0.081715
INFO:tensorflow:2018-06-21 12:10:52.459310: Step 499: Validation accuracy = 93.0
% (N=100)
INFO:tensorflow:Final test accuracy = 89.5% (N=664)
INFO:tensorflow:Froze 2 variables.
Converted 2 variables to const ops.

(project) D:\Users\vavinas\tensorflow-for-poets-2>
(project) D:\Users\vavinas\tensorflow-for-poets-2>
```

About bottlenecks

Here, we will try to understand how the retraining process works. The ImageNet models we are using are made up of many layers stacked on top of each other. These layers are pre-trained and already have sufficient information that will help in image classification. All we are trying to do is train the very last layer, `final_training_ops` , when all the previous layers retrain their already trained state.

The following screenshot is taken from TensorBoard. You can open TensorBoard in your browser to get a better look at it. You will find it in the **Graphs** tab:

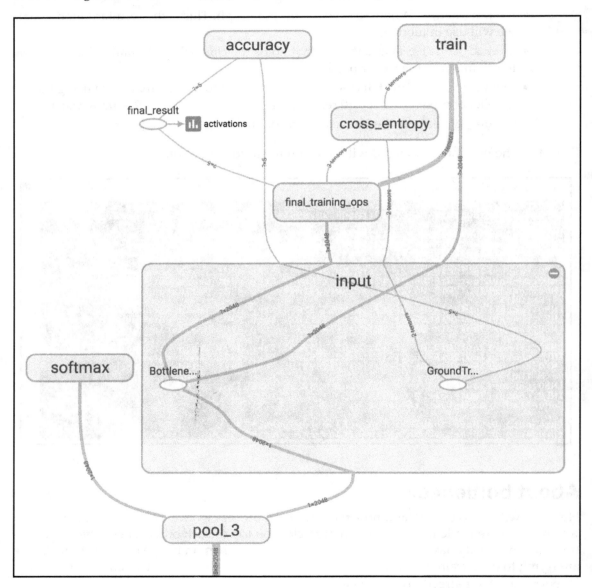

In the preceding diagram, the **softmax** node on the left-hand side is the output layer of the original model. All the nodes to the right of **softmax** were added by the retraining script.

> Note that this will only work after the retrain script finishes generating the **bottleneck** files.

Bottleneck is the term used to refer to the layer just before the final output layer that does the classification. Bottleneck does not imply its conventional meaning of something that slows down the whole process. We use the term bottleneck because, near the output, the representation is much more compact than in the main body of the network.

Every image is reused multiple times during training. Calculating the layers behind the bottleneck for each image takes a significant amount of time. Since these lower layers of the network are not being modified, their output can be cached and reused. Now, you have the TensorFlow retrained model in your hand. Let's test the model that we just trained using the following command:

```
python -m scripts.label_image \
    --graph=tf_files/retrained_graph.pb  \
    --image=tf_files\food_photos\pizza\1.jpg
```

Executing the previous code block will give you the class that the food image belongs to. Now, let's go to the next task: converting the tensorflow model into the Core ML format.

Converting the TensorFlow model into the Core ML model

The TensorFlow team has developed a package that is used to convert the models created in TensorFlow into Core ML, which in through is used in iOS apps. To use this, you must have macOS with Python 3.6 and TensorFlow installed. Using this, we can convert the TensorFlow model file (.pb) into the Core ML format (.mlmodel). First, you need to execute the following command:

```
Pip install tfcoreml
```

Once this is installed, write the following code in your Python file, name it `inspect.py`, and save it:

```python
import tensorflow as tf
from tensorflow.core.framework import graph_pb2
import time
import operator
import sys

def inspect(model_pb, output_txt_file):
    graph_def = graph_pb2.GraphDef()
    with open(model_pb, "rb") as f:
        graph_def.ParseFromString(f.read())

    tf.import_graph_def(graph_def)

    sess = tf.Session()
    OPS = sess.graph.get_operations()

    ops_dict = {}

    sys.stdout = open(output_txt_file, 'w')
    for i, op in enumerate(OPS):
        print('----------------------------------------------------------------------------------------------------------------')
        print("{}: op name = {}, op type = ( {} ), inputs = {}, outputs = {}".format(i, op.name, op.type, ", ".join([x.name for x in op.inputs]), ", ".join([x.name for x in op.outputs])))
        print('@input shapes:')
        for x in op.inputs:
            print("name = {} : {}".format(x.name, x.get_shape()))
        print('@output shapes:')
        for x in op.outputs:
            print("name = {} : {}".format(x.name, x.get_shape()))
        if op.type in ops_dict:
            ops_dict[op.type] += 1
        else:
            ops_dict[op.type] = 1

    print('----------------------------------------------------------------------------------------------------------------')
    sorted_ops_count = sorted(ops_dict.items(), key=operator.itemgetter(1))
    print('OPS counts:')
    for i in sorted_ops_count:
        print("{} : {}".format(i[0], i[1]))
```

```
if __name__ == "__main__":
    """
    Write a summary of the frozen TF graph to a text file.
    Summary includes op name, type, input and output names and shapes.

    Arguments
    ----------
    - path to the frozen .pb graph
    - path to the output .txt file where the summary is written

    Usage
    ----------
    python inspect_pb.py frozen.pb text_file.txt

    """
    if len(sys.argv) != 3:
        raise ValueError("Script expects two arguments. " +
                "Usage: python inspect_pb.py /path/to/the/frozen.pb
/path/to/the/output/text/file.txt")
    inspect(sys.argv[1], sys.argv[2])
```

The preceding code will take the model file as an input argument, and save all the operations and input/output node names with a description in a text file that we supply as input. To run this, enter the following command:

Python inspect.py retrained_graph.pb summeries.txt

In this command, you are executing the inspect.py code you saved before. This will also input the graph file obtained from the previous section and, path of a text file where you want to save the summaries.

Once you execute this command, `summeries.txt` will be created with all the summaries, as shown here. These will be added into that file:

```
0: op name = import/final_training_ops/biases/final_biases, op type = ( Const ), inputs = , outputs = import/final_traini
@input shapes:
@output shapes:
name = import/final_training_ops/biases/final_biases:0 : (5,)

1: op name = import/final_training_ops/biases/final_biases/read, op type = ( Identity ), inputs = import/final_training_op
@input shapes:
name = import/final_training_ops/biases/final_biases:0 : (5,)
@output shapes:
name = import/final_training_ops/biases/final_biases/read:0 : (5,)

2: op name = import/final_training_ops/weights/final_weights, op type = ( Const ), inputs = , outputs = import/final_train
@input shapes:
@output shapes:
name = import/final_training_ops/weights/final_weights:0 : (1001, 5)

3: op name = import/final_training_ops/weights/final_weights/read, op type = ( Identity ), inputs = import/final_training_
@input shapes:
name = import/final_training_ops/weights/final_weights:0 : (1001, 5)
@output shapes:
name = import/final_training_ops/weights/final_weights/read:0 : (1001, 5)

4: op name = import/input, op type = ( Placeholder ), inputs = , outputs = import/input:0
@input shapes:
@output shapes:
name = import/input:0 : (1, 224, 224, 3)

5: op name = import/MobilenetV1/Conv2d_0/weights, op type = ( Const ), inputs = , outputs = import/MobilenetV1/Conv2d_0/we
@input shapes:
@output shapes:
name = import/MobilenetV1/Conv2d_0/weights:0 : (3, 3, 3, 16)
```

In this file, you can see all the operations, input and output names, and their shapes; you can also see the overall operators:

```
OPS counts:
Placeholder : 1
AvgPool : 1
BiasAdd : 1
Squeeze : 1
Reshape : 1
PlaceholderWithDefault : 1
MatMul : 1
Softmax : 1
DepthwiseConv2dNative : 13
Conv2D : 15
Rsqrt : 27
Sub : 27
Relu6 : 27
Add : 55
Mul : 81
Identity : 140
Const : 167
```

Toward the end of the file, you will find the definition of the end node; in our case, it is as follows:

```
559: op name = import/final_result, op type = ( Softmax ), inputs = import/final_training_ops/Wx_plus_b/add:0, outputs = import/final_result:0
@input shapes:
name = import/final_training_ops/Wx_plus_b/add:0 : (?, 5)
@output shapes:
name = import/final_result:0 : (?, 5)
```

Here, you can see that the end node operation type is `Softmax`, and the output that it will produce will be stored in the `final_result:0` name. Now, check out the following code block, which is used to generate a corresponding Core ML model:

```
import tfcoreml as tf_converter
tf_converter.convert(tf_model_path = 'retrained_graph.pb',
                     mlmodel_path = 'converted.mlmodel',
                     output_feature_names = ['final_result:0'],
                     image_input_names = 'input:0',
                     class_labels = 'retrained_labels.txt',
                     red_bias = -1,
                     green_bias = -1,
                     blue_bias = -1,
                     image_scale = 2.0/224.0
                     )
```

Let's understand the previous code block in detail. You must have noticed that we imported the `tfcoreml` package in the first line, and then used its **convert** function. The following are its arguments:

- `Tf_model_path`: The (`.pb`) file path that you generated in the previous section, *Converting the TensorFlow model into the Core ML model*.
- `Mlmodel_path`: The output model file path where you want to generate the model.
- `Output_feature_names`: In this, we will get the output variable name that you obtained from the previous text file that was generated by our model-inspection code.
- `Image_input_names`: Name you want to give for the image input. In Core ML/iOS, this will be the image buffer.
- `Class_labels`: This is the file you will get in the training step.

Once you run the preceding code, you will see the generated `converted.mlmodel` file in your directory. You can import this into your Xcode project and make use of it.

Writing the iOS mobile application

In this section, we are going to create an app to make use of the image recognition model that we've created to predict images using your iOS mobile camera.

To start, you need a Mac PC running Xcode version 9+. Download the source code (x-code project) from the Git repository and navigate to the project folder. Open the `recognition.xcodeproj` image in Xcode. The following screenshot shows the folder structure of the project:

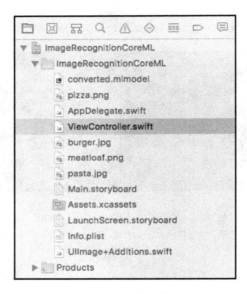

The main file we are going to view is `controller.swift`. It contains the following code:

```swift
import UIKit
class ViewController: UIViewController {
    @IBOutlet weak var pictureImageView :UIImageView!
    @IBOutlet weak var titleLabel :UILabel!
```

These are the outlets for the image-view control and title-label control in the main storyboard:

```
private var model : converted = converted()
```

This is the instance of the model that was generated when we added the `core-ml` file we created in the previous section:

```
var content : [ String : String ] = [
    "cheeseburger" : "A cheeseburger is a hamburger topped with cheese.
Traditionally, the slice of cheese is placed on top of the meat patty, but
the burger can include many variations in structure, ingredients, and
composition.\nIt has 303 calories per 100 grams.",
    "carbonara" : "Carbonara is an Italian pasta dish from Rome made
with egg, hard cheese, guanciale, and pepper. The recipe is not fixed by a
specific type of hard cheese or pasta. The cheese is usually Pecorino
Romano.",
    "meat loaf" : "Meatloaf is a dish of ground meat mixed with other
ingredients and formed into a loaf shape, then baked or smoked. The shape
is created by either cooking it in a loaf pan, or forming it by hand on a
flat pan.\nIt has 149 calories / 100 grams",
    "pizza" : "Pizza is a traditional Italian dish consisting of a
yeasted flatbread typically topped with tomato sauce and cheese and baked
in an oven. It can also be topped with additional vegetables, meats, and
condiments, and can be made without cheese.\nIt has 285 calories / 100
grams"
]
```

We hardcoded the contents to display in the title label for the corresponding class label we trained:

```
let images = ["burger.jpg","pizza.png", "pasta.jpg","meatloaf.png"]
```

These are the images we have added to the project; they'll serve as input for our prediction app:

```
var index = 0
override func viewDidLoad() {
    super.viewDidLoad()
    nextImage()
}
@IBAction func nextButtonPressed() {
    nextImage()
}
func nextImage() {
    defer { index = index < images.count - 1 ? index + 1 : 0 }
    let filename = images[index]
    guard let img = UIImage(named: filename) else {
```

```
        self.titleLabel.text = "Failed to load image \(filename)"
        return
    }
    self.pictureImageView.image = img
    let resizedImage = img.resizeTo(size: CGSize(width: 224, height:
224))
    guard let buffer = resizedImage.toBuffer() else {
        self.titleLabel.text = "Failed to make buffer from image
\(filename)"
        return
    }
```

As we trained our model with 224 px images, we are also resizing the images of the input and converting it into an image buffer, which we want to give to the prediction method:

```
    do {
        let prediction = try self.model.prediction(input:
MymodelInput(input__0: buffer))
```

Here, we are inputting the image and getting the prediction results:

```
        if content.keys.contains(prediction.classLabel) {
            self.titleLabel.text = content[prediction.classLabel]
        }
        else
        {
            self.titleLabel.text = prediction.classLabel;
        }
```

In the preceding code, depending on the class label, we are displaying the content to the user:

```
    } catch let error {
        self.titleLabel.text = error.localizedDescription
    }
  }
}
```

This completes the application's creation. Now, we will execute the application to find the following images as output:

Click on **Next** to find the our next image:

Handwritten digit recognition solution

Previously, we created an application that helped us get insights into the implementation of a neural network image recognition program using the TensorFlow model for mobile devices. Now, we will create another application that uses the concept of a neural network and Keras for an image recognition program of handwritten digits. In this section, we will create an application for a handwritten digit recognition solution on mobile devices using Keras. Then, we will convert this Keras model into a Core ML model and use it to build an iOS mobile application. Let's start by introducing you to Keras.

Introduction to Keras

Keras is a high-level neural network API, written in Python and capable of running on top of TensorFlow, CNTK, or Theano. It was developed with the aim of enabling fast experimentation.

Here are some of the key uses of Keras:

- Allows for easy and fast prototyping (through user-friendliness, modularity, and extensibility)
- Supports both convolutional networks and recurrent networks, as well as a combination of the two
- Runs seamlessly on CPU and GPU

Keras was designed on the following principles:

- User-friendliness
- Modularity
- Easy extensibility
- Compatibility with Python

To learn more about Keras, check out https://keras.io/.

Installing Keras

As we already discussed, Keras doesn't have its own backend system. As it is running on top of TensorFlow, CNTK, or Theano, we need to install one of these—personally, we recommend TensorFlow.

We need to install the h5py library, with the help of the pip package manager, in order to save the Keras models to disk:

```
pip install tensorflow
pip install keras
pip install h5py
```

The preceding commands will install the basic required libraries for the model, which we are going to create now.

Solving the problem

In this section, we are going to see a practical implementation of a neural network. We will define the problem statement, then we will understand the dataset we are going to use to solve the problem, whereupon we will create the model in Keras to solve the problem. Once the model is created in Keras, we will convert it into a model that's compatible with Core ML. This Core ML model will be imported into an iOS application, and a program will be written to use this model and interpret the handwritten digits.

Defining the problem statement

We are going to tackle the problem of recognizing handwritten digits through a machine learning model that we'll implement in an iOS mobile application. The first step is to have the database of handwritten digits that can be used for model training and testing.

The MNIST digits dataset (`http://yann.lecun.com/exdb/mnist/`) provides a database of handwritten digits, and has a training set of 60,000 examples and a test set of 10,000 examples. It is a subset of a larger set that's available from MNIST. The digits have been size-normalized and centered in a fixed-size image. It is a good database for people who want to learn techniques and pattern recognition methods on real-world data while exerting minimal effort on preprocessing and formatting.

Before solving this problem, we will spend some time understanding the problem to see where the neural network can help. We can split the problem of recognizing handwritten digits into two sub-problems. Suppose we are given a handwritten number, as follows:

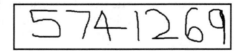

First, we need to break an image containing many digits into a sequence of separate images, each containing a single digit. For example, we'd like to break this image into seven separate images, as shown here:

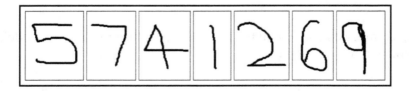

For humans, the digits can be easily separated, but it is very challenging for machines to do this simple task. Once the digits are separated, the program needs to classify each individual digit. So, for instance, we'd like our program to recognize that the first digit is a **5**.

We are now trying to focus on the second part of the problem: to recognize the individual digits and classify them. We are going to use a neural network to solve the problem of recognizing individual, handwritten digits.

We can solve this problem using a 3-layer neural network, with the output layers having 10 neurons. The input layer and the hidden layers are where the processing happens. in the output layer, based on the neuron that fires, we can easily infer the digit that was recognized. Neurons 0 to 9 each identify one digit.

Problem solution

The problem solution consists of the following key steps:

1. Preparing the data
2. Defining the model
3. Training and fitting the model
4. Converting the trained Keras model into a Core ML model
5. Writing the iOS mobile application

Now, let's go through the steps one by one and see what we need to do in each of these steps.

Preparing the data

The first activity is the data preparation. To start, let's import all the required libraries. As we discussed earlier, we are going to use the MNIST database for the dataset of handwritten digits:

```
from __future__ import print_function
from matplotlib import pyplot as plt
import keras
from keras.datasets import mnist
```

`mnist` is the dataset that contains the handwritten digits database, so we need to import that, as follows:

```
from keras.models import Sequential
```

The preceding code imports the `Sequential` model type from Keras. This is simply a linear stack of neural network layers:

```
from keras.layers import Dense, Dropout, Flatten
```

Now, we need to import the core layers from Keras. These are the layers that are used in almost any neural network:

```
from keras.layers import Conv2D, MaxPooling2D
```

Import the CNN layers from Keras. These are the convolutional layers that will help us efficiently train on image data:

```
from keras.utils import np_utils
```

Import Utils. This will help us do data transformation later:

```
from keras import backend as K
import coremltools
```

`coremltools` will help us convert the Keras model into the Core ML model:

```
(x_train, y_train), (x_val, y_val) = mnist.load_data()
```

Load the pre-shuffled MNIST data into train and test sets:

```
# Inspect x data
print('x_train shape: ', x_train.shape)
print(x_train.shape[0], 'training samples')
print('x_val shape: ', x_val.shape)
print(x_val.shape[0], 'validation samples')
print('First x sample\n', x_train[0])
```

If you run the preceding code, it will show the shape of X, Y, and also the first record of X.

So, we have 60,000 samples in our training set, and the images are 28 x 28 pixels each. We can confirm this by plotting the first sample in `matplotlib`:

```
conv.py [D:\Users\vavinash\PycharmProjects\mlfacedettection\Scripts\python.exe]
Using TensorFlow backend.
WARNING:root:TensorFlow version 1.12.0 detected. Last version known to be fully co
keras version  2.1.6
x_train shape:  (60000, 28, 28)
60000 training samples
x_val shape:  (10000, 28, 28)
10000 validation samples
First x sample
[[ 0    0    0    0    0    0    0    0    0    0    0    0    0    0    0    0    0    0
   0    0    0    0    0    0    0    0    0    0]
 [ 0    0    0    0    0    0    0    0    0    0    0    0    0    0    0    0    0    0
   0    0    0    0    0    0    0    0    0    0]
 [ 0    0    0    0    0    0    0    0    0    0    0    0    0    0    0    0    0    0
   0    0    0    0    0    0    0    0    0    0]
 [ 0    0    0    0    0    0    0    0    0    0    0    0    0    0    0    0    0    0
   0    0    0    0    0    0    0    0    0    0]
 [ 0    0    0    0    0    0    0    0    0    0    0    0    0    0    0    0    0    0
   0    0    0    0    0    0    0    0    0    0]
 [ 0    0    0    0    0    0    0    0    0    0    0    0    3   18   18   18  126  136
 175   26  166  255  247  127    0    0    0    0]
 [ 0    0    0    0    0    0    0    0   30   36   94  154  170  253  253  253  253  253
 225  172  253  242  195   64    0    0    0    0]
```

plt.imshow(x_train[0])

This statement will use the matplotlib library to plot the first record of x_train, which will give the following output:

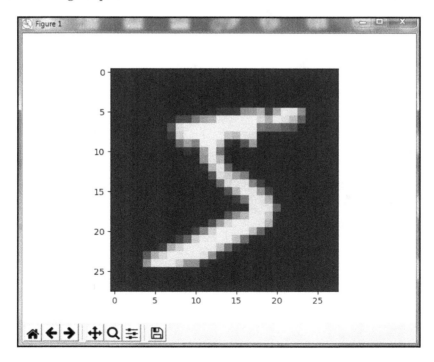

The following lines will print the `y_train` shape and the first 10 elements in `y_train`:

```
print('y_train shape: ', y_train.shape)
print('First 10 y_train elements:', y_train[:10])
```

The following code will find the input shape of the image. The MNIST image data values are of the `uint8` type, in the *[0, 255]* range, but Keras needs values of the `float32` type in the *[0, 1]* range:

```
img_rows, img_cols = x_train.shape[1], x_train.shape[2]
num_classes = 10

# Set input_shape for channels_first or channels_last
if K.image_data_format() == 'channels_first':
x_train = x_train.reshape(x_train.shape[0], 1, img_rows, img_cols)
x_val = x_val.reshape(x_val.shape[0], 1, img_rows, img_cols)
input_shape = (1, img_rows, img_cols)
else:
    x_train = x_train.reshape(x_train.shape[0], img_rows, img_cols, 1)
    x_val = x_val.reshape(x_val.shape[0], img_rows, img_cols, 1)
    input_shape = (img_rows, img_cols, 1)

print('x_train shape:', x_train.shape)
# x_train shape: (60000, 28, 28, 1)
print('x_val shape:', x_val.shape)
# x_val shape: (10000, 28, 28, 1)
print('input_shape:', input_shape)
```

Using the following code, we are converting the datatype to be compatible with the datatype that is defined in Keras:

```
x_train = x_train.astype('float32')
x_val = x_val.astype('float32')
x_train /= 255
x_val /= 255
```

Now, we have a one-dimensional of 60,000 elements in y. Let's convert it into a 60,000 x 10 array, as follows:

```
y_train = np_utils.to_categorical(y_train, num_classes)
y_val = np_utils.to_categorical(y_val, num_classes)
print('New y_train shape: ', y_train.shape)
# (60000, 10)
print('New y_train shape: ', y_train.shape)
# (60000, 10)
print('First 10 y_train elements, reshaped:\n', y_train[:10])
```

Now, y_train will look like this:

```
[[0. 0. 0. 0. 0. 1. 0. 0. 0. 0.]
 [1. 0. 0. 0. 0. 0. 0. 0. 0. 0.]
 [0. 0. 0. 0. 1. 0. 0. 0. 0. 0.]
 [0. 1. 0. 0. 0. 0. 0. 0. 0. 0.]
 [0. 0. 0. 0. 0. 0. 0. 0. 0. 1.]
 [0. 0. 1. 0. 0. 0. 0. 0. 0. 0.]
 [0. 1. 0. 0. 0. 0. 0. 0. 0. 0.]
 [0. 0. 0. 1. 0. 0. 0. 0. 0. 0.]
 [0. 1. 0. 0. 0. 0. 0. 0. 0. 0.]
 [0. 0. 0. 0. 1. 0. 0. 0. 0. 0.]]
```

In the preceding array, we can find that for the presence of digits, the corresponding position will be filled with 1—all others will be filled with 0. For the first record, we can understand that the predicted digit is 5, because the 6th position (starting from 0) was filled with 1.

Now that the data preparation is complete, we need to define the model's architecture.

Defining the model's architecture

Once the data preparation is completed, the next step is to define the model and create it, so let's create the model:

```
model_m = Sequential()
```

The preceding line will create a sequential model that will process the layers in the sequential way they are arranged. There are two ways to build Keras models, sequential and functional:

- **The sequential API**: This allows us to create models layer-by-layer. Through this, we cannot create models that share layers or have multiple input or output.
- **The functional API**: This allows us to create models that are more than and can have complex connection layers—you can literally connect from any layer to any other layer:

```
model_m.add(Conv2D(32, (5, 5), input_shape=(1,28,28),
activation='relu'))
```

The input shape parameter should be the shape of 1 sample. In this case, it's the same `(1, 28, 28)`, which corresponds to the (depth, width, height) of each digit image.

But what do the other parameters represent? They correspond to the number of convolutional filters to use, the number of rows in each convolution kernel, and the number of columns in each convolution kernel, respectively:

```
model_m.add(MaxPooling2D(pool_size=(2, 2)))
```

`MaxPooling2D` is a way to reduce the number of parameters in our model by sliding a 2 x 2 pooling filter across the previous layer and taking the max of the 4 values in the 2 x 2 filter:

```
model_m.add(Dropout(0.5))
```

This is a method for regularizing our model in order to prevent overfitting:

```
model_m.add(Conv2D(64, (3, 3), activation='relu'))
model_m.add(MaxPooling2D(pool_size=(2, 2)))
model_m.add(Dropout(0.2))
model_m.add(Conv2D(128, (1, 1), activation='relu'))
model_m.add(MaxPooling2D(pool_size=(2, 2)))
model_m.add(Dropout(0.2))
model_m.add(Flatten())
model_m.add(Dense(128, activation='relu'))
model_m.add(Dense(num_classes, activation='softmax'))
print(model_m.summary())
```

Once you run the preceding lines of code, the model architecture's names of the layers will be printed in the console:

```
Layer (type)                    Output Shape            Param #
=================================================================
conv2d_1 (Conv2D)               (None, 24, 24, 32)      832
_____
max_pooling2d_1 (MaxPooling2    (None, 12, 12, 32)      0
_____
dropout_1 (Dropout)             (None, 12, 12, 32)      0
_____
conv2d_2 (Conv2D)               (None, 10, 10, 64)      18496
_____
max_pooling2d_2 (MaxPooling2    (None, 5, 5, 64)        0
_____
dropout_2 (Dropout)             (None, 5, 5, 64)        0
_____
conv2d_3 (Conv2D)               (None, 5, 5, 128)       8320
_____
max_pooling2d_3 (MaxPooling2    (None, 2, 2, 128)       0
_____
dropout_3 (Dropout)             (None, 2, 2, 128)       0
_____
flatten_1 (Flatten)             (None, 512)             0
_____
dense_1 (Dense)                 (None, 128)             65664
_____
dense_2 (Dense)                 (None, 10)              1290
=================================================================
Total params: 94,602
Trainable params: 94,602
Non-trainable params: 0
```

Compiling and fitting the model

The next step is to compile and train the model. We put the model through the training phase with a series of iterations. Epochs determine the number of iterations to be done on a model in the training phase. The weights will be passed to the layers defined in the model. A good number of Epochs will give greater accuracy and minimum loss. Here, we are using 10 Epochs.

Keras has a callback mechanism that will be called during each training iteration of the model, that is, at the end of each Epoch. In the callback method, we save the computed weights of that Epoch:

```
callbacks_list = [
    keras.callbacks.ModelCheckpoint(
        filepath='best_model.{epoch:02d}-{val_loss:.2f}.h5',
        monitor='val_loss', save_best_only=True),
    keras.callbacks.EarlyStopping(monitor='acc', patience=1)]
```

Now, compile the model using the following code:

```
model_m.compile(loss='categorical_crossentropy',optimizer='adam',
metrics=['accuracy'])
```

The `categorical_crossentropy` loss function measures the distance between the probability distribution calculated by the CNN, and the true distribution of the labels.

An `optimizer` is the stochastic gradient descent algorithm that tries to minimize the loss function by following the gradient at just the right speed. `accuracy` the fraction of the images that were correctly classified—this is the most common metric monitored during training and testing:

```
# Hyper-parameters
batch_size = 200
epochs = 10
```

Now, fit the model using the following code:

```
# Enable validation to use ModelCheckpoint and EarlyStopping
callbacks.model_m.fit(
    x_train, y_train, batch_size=batch_size, epochs=epochs,
callbacks=callbacks_list, validation_data=(x_val, y_val), verbose=1)
```

Once the program finishes executing, you will find files in your running directory with the `best_model.01-0.15.h5` name. This states `best_model.{epoch number}-{loss value}.h5`.

This the Keras model that was created and trained for the given dataset.

Converting the Keras model into the Core ML model

Now that the Keras model has been created, the next step is to convert the Keras model into the Core ML model. For the first argument, use the filename of the newest `.h5` file in the notebook folder:

```
output_labels = ['0', '1', '2', '3', '4', '5', '6', '7', '8', '9']
coreml_mnist = coremltools.converters.keras.convert(
    'best_model.10-0.04.h5', input_names=['image'],
output_names=['output'],    class_labels=output_labels,
image_input_names='image')
coreml_mnist.save("minsit_classifier.mlmodel")
```

Once you successfully run the code, you will find the `minsit_classifer.mlmodel` file created in your directory. We are going to use this to create an iOS mobile application to detect the digits.

Creating the iOS mobile application

Now, we are going to create the iOS app. You can download the code from our Packt GitHub repository in the `ImageClassificationwithVisionandCoreML` folder.

Open the project in Xcode9+; the project structure will look like this:

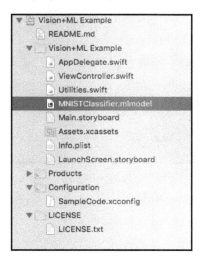

If you open `main.storyboard` in your designer, you will see the following UI:

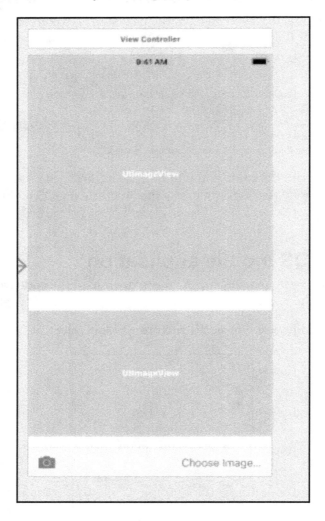

Most code is common iOS code. Check out the following piece of code, which is of specific interest to us, and includes the handwritten digit prediction code:

```
lazy var classificationRequest: VNCoreMLRequest = {
        // Load the ML model through its generated class and create a
Vision request for it.
        do {
            let model = try VNCoreMLModel(for: MNISTClassifier().model)
            return VNCoreMLRequest(model: model, completionHandler:
self.handleClassification)
        } catch {
            fatalError("can't load Vision ML model: \(error)")
        }
    }()
    func handleClassification(request: VNRequest, error: Error?) {
        guard let observations = request.results as?
[VNClassificationObservation]
            else { fatalError("unexpected result type from
VNCoreMLRequest") }
        guard let best = observations.first
            else { fatalError("can't get best result") }
DispatchQueue.main.async {
            self.classificationLabel.text = "Classification:
\"\(best.identifier)\" Confidence: \(best.confidence)"
        }
    }
```

It contains two buttons at the bottom: one to pick an image from mobile and another option to take a snapshot. Please note that the camera will not work if you are running this in simulators.

You can build and run the app in a simulator. Once the app successfully opens in a simulator, drag the image of the handwritten digit 6 into the folder example image into the simulator–this will save the file in the simulator's memory.

Return to the app and select the dragged image that was saved in the device's memory. It will show the following output:

Summary

In this chapter, we covered the concept of neural networks and their use in the field of mobile machine learning. We created an application to recognize images using TensorFlow and Core ML in iOS and Xcode. We also explored the Keras deep learning framework. We tried to solve the handwritten digit recognition problem using a neural network in Keras. We built the Keras machine learning model to solve this problem. Then, we converted this model into a Core ML model using Core ML conversion tools. We used this Core ML model in an iOS mobile application to perform the handwritten digit recognition.

In the next chapter, we will learn how to use the Google Cloud Vision label detection technique in Android.

10
Mobile Application Using Google Vision

As we saw in Chapter 1, *Introduction to Machine Learning on Mobile,* we know that machine learning in mobile applications can be implemented either on-device or it can be implemented using machine learning cloud provider services. There are various machine learning cloud providers:

- Clarifai
- Google Cloud Vision
- Microsoft Azure Cognitive Services
- IBM Watson
- Amazon Machine Learning

In this chapter, we are going to dive deeply into Google Cloud Vision to understand the following:

- Features of Google Cloud Vision
- How to utilize the Google Cloud Vision label-detection technique in an Android Mobile application to determine what is the picture taken by the camera. That is, we basically feed an image into Google Cloud Vision and see how it labels the image. Google Vision is going to predict the image that it receives from the mobile application and provide a label for the image.

Features of Google Cloud Vision

Google Cloud Vision API comprises various complex and powerful machine learning models that help to perform image analysis. It classifies images into various categories using an easy-to-use REST API. The important features provided by Google Cloud Vision include the following:

- **Label detection**: This enables us to classify images into thousands of categories. The images can be categorized into various common category labels, such as *animals* and *fruits*.
- **Image attribute detection**: This enables us to detect individual objects from within images. It can also detect attributes such as prominent color.
- **Face detection**: This enables us to detect faces from within images. If there are multiple faces in the images, each can be detected individually. It can also detect the prominent attributes associated with a face, such as wearing a helmet.
- **Logo detection**: This enables us to detect printed words from images. Prominent logos are trained which can be detected.
- **Landmark detection**: It is trained to detect prominent landmarks – natural and man-made–so these are detected through Google Vision.
- **Optical character recognition**: This helps to detect the text within images even if they aren't in English. This supports a wide range of languages.
- **Explicit content detection**: This helps to identify the type of content or sentiment of the content, such as *violent* or *humorous*. It enables us to perform sentiment analysis of images by leveraging the metadata information that can be built.
- **Search web**: This searches the web for similar images.

All these features provided by Google Cloud Vision can be used by invoking simple RESTful APIs provided by Google. However, for their use, there is a price attached to using each feature. A combination of features can also be used. The pricing details can be found on the Google Cloud Vision website: `https://cloud.google.com/vision/`.

Sample mobile application using Google Cloud Vision

In this section, we are going to try a sample Android mobile application using Google Cloud Vision. We are going to capture an image from the camera of the cell phone, upload the image to Google Cloud Vision, and see what it predicts the image to be. This is going to use the label detection feature of Google Cloud Vision, which determines the label of the uploaded image.

How does label detection work?

The Vision API can detect and extract information about entities within an image, across a broad group of categories. Labels can identify objects, locations, activities, animal species, products, and more. Labels are returned in English only.

The image whose label is to be determined and the features of the Google Vision that we intend to use needs to be sent in the request API. The feature can be any of the features listed in the *Features of Google Cloud Vision* section, such as label detection or logo detection. If there is any additional image context that needs to be sent across along with the image, it can be sent as an additional parameter. The request API JSON format is provided here:

```
{
  "image": {
    object(Image)// Image which needs to be processed.
  },
  "features": [
    {
      object(Feature) //Google Vision Feature that needs to be invoked.
    }
  ],
  "imageContext": {
    object(ImageContext) //additional image context if required.
  },
}
```

The image object can be a base64-encoded string or it can be a URL of the image that needs to be analyzed. The URL can be a Google Cloud Storage image location, or a publicly accessible image URL.

The response for the request is going to be a list of annotations based on the features requested. In our case, it is going to be label annotations:

```
{
 "labelAnnotations": [
 {
 object(EntityAnnotation)
 }
 ],
 "error": {
 object(Status)
 },
}
```

The returned `EntityAnnotation` object is going to contain the label of the image, the prediction score, and other useful information. All labels that match the input image object are returned as an array list with the prediction score, based on which we could perform the required inference needed in our application.

Now that we understand the basics of how label detection works, let's start creating the Android application.

Prerequisites

In order to get started start exploring the Google Vision and to write a program using the services exposed by Google vision, the following are required to be setup, so we can get our hands dirty:

- A Google Cloud Platform account
- A Project on Google Cloud Console
- The latest version of Android Studio
- A mobile phone running Android 5.0 or higher

Preparations

This section gives details about the key activities we need to do before we can start using the Google Cloud Vision API from our mobile application:

1. The Google Cloud Vision API should be enabled in the Google Cloud Console and an API key should be created that will be used in the mobile application code. Please perform the following steps to get the Cloud Vision API key:

    1. Open `cloud.google.com/vision`.
    2. Go to Console. If you do no have a trial account, it will ask you to create one and complete the process.
    3. Enable billing so we get $300 free credit. Once we have the account, we can go to Console and complete the process of creating the key.
    4. From the Console, create a project.
    5. Open that project. Go to **API services | Library search for cloud vision API**.
    6. Click on it and enable it.
    7. Go to **API Services | Credentials**.
    8. Go to **Credentials | API Key**.
    9. Create the API key.
    10. Copy the API key; this will be used in the mobile application code.

2. Add the dependencies required in the mobile client application to use the Google Cloud Vision API. The Google API Client will be needed and hence this needs to be added to the client project. These will need to be specified in the Gradle build file. The sample Gradle file with the key dependencies is as follows:

```
dependencies {
 compile fileTree(include: ['*.jar'], dir: 'libs')
 testCompile 'junit:junit:4.12'
 compile 'com.android.support:appcompat-v7:27.0.2'
 compile 'com.android.support:design:27.0.2'
 compile 'com.google.api-client:google-api-client-android:1.23.0'
exclude module: 'httpclient'
 compile 'com.google.http-client:google-http-client-gson:1.23.0'
exclude module: 'httpclient'
 compile 'com.google.apis:google-api-services-vision:v1-
rev369-1.23.0'
 }
```

Understanding the Application

In this section, we will see the key flows of the source code to understand how the Google Vision API works from an Android mobile application.

The Vision class represents the Google API Client for Cloud Vision. The first step is to initialize the Vision class. We do it through the Builder, to which we specify the transport mechanism and the JSON factory to be used:

```
Vision.Builder builder = new Vision.Builder(httpTransport, jsonFactory, null);
```

The next step is to assign the API key to the Vision Builder so it can start interacting with the cloud APIs. The key we have created is given here:

```
VisionRequestInitializer requestInitializer = new
VisionRequestInitializer(CLOUD_VISION_API_KEY)
builder.setVisionRequestInitializer(requestInitializer);
```

The final step is to get the Vision instance through which the cloud APIs can be invoked:

```
Vision vision = builder.build();
```

Now we are going to capture a picture and send the picture to the cloud API to detect its label. The code to capture the picture through the camera is the usual Android stuff. The following code provides details on how the image is converted into a Vision Request for label detection:

```
BatchAnnotateImagesRequest batchAnnotateImagesRequest = new
BatchAnnotateImagesRequest();

batchAnnotateImagesRequest.setRequests(new
ArrayList<AnnotateImageRequest>() {{ AnnotateImageRequest
annotateImageRequest = new AnnotateImageRequest();
 // Add the image
 Image base64EncodedImage = new Image();
 // Convert the bitmap to a JPEG
 // Just in case it's a format that Android understands but Cloud Vision
 ByteArrayOutputStream byteArrayOutputStream = new ByteArrayOutputStream();
bitmap.compress(Bitmap.CompressFormat.JPEG, 90, byteArrayOutputStream);
byte[] imageBytes = byteArrayOutputStream.toByteArray();
 // Base64 encode the JPEG
base64EncodedImage.encodeContent(imageBytes);
annotateImageRequest.setImage(base64EncodedImage);
 // add the features we want
annotateImageRequest.setFeatures(new ArrayList<Feature>() {{
Feature labelDetection = new Feature();
```

```
labelDetection.setType("LABEL_DETECTION");
labelDetection.setMaxResults(MAX_LABEL_RESULTS);
add(labelDetection);
}});
// Add the list of one thing to the request
add(annotateImageRequest);
}});
Vision.Images.Annotate annotateRequest =
vision.images().annotate(batchAnnotateImagesRequest);
```

Google Cloud Vision will be called as an **async task**. The response received from the API will be analyzed to provide data in user-readable format. The following code provides details of the response received from Google Vision:

```
//Formatting the response as a string
 private static String convertResponseToString(BatchAnnotateImagesResponse
response) {
 StringBuilder message = new StringBuilder("I found these things:\n\n");
List<EntityAnnotation> labels =
response.getResponses().get(0).getLabelAnnotations();
 if (labels != null) {
 for (EntityAnnotation label : labels) {
 message.append(String.format(Locale.US, "%.3f: %s", label.getScore(),
label.getDescription()));
 message.append("\n");
 }
 } else {
 message.append("nothing");
 }
 return message.toString();
 }
```

The labels returned for the image can be viewed by the user.

Output

This section displays the Android application screen when a mobile phone has been captured and sent to the vision API. Possible labels are listed in the output screen:

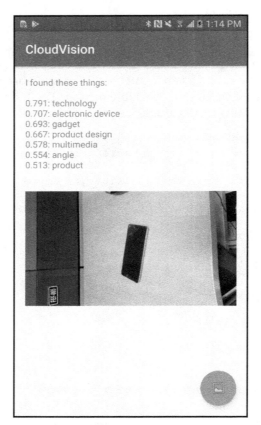

Summary

In this chapter, we looked at how Google Cloud Vision works, and can how to invoke it from a mobile application without much effort. We saw how easy it is to make complex machine learning predictions without the hassles of model selection and training. In the next chapter, we will explore the future of machine learning in the field of mobile applications.

11
The Future of ML on Mobile Applications

Machine learning (**ML**) requires massive computational power and, hence, requires specialized processors. But if the power of ML can be brought to mobile devices that lack such processing power and also work in offline mode, there will be enormous opportunities and an entire new business category with a whole gamut of innovative useful mobile applications that are very hard to imagine otherwise. The entire way customers and businesses connect with each other would be reshaped.

Mobile devices have become extended organs of human beings these days. It is hard to find anyone without a mobile phone with them always. If a mobile phone is going to be a part of the human being, then, just as the eyes, nose, legs, and so on know what we do daily and have got accustomed to our lifestyle, in a similar manner, mobile phones can also understand the ins and outs of our daily routine and can bring out so many key data points, which we may not have had the time to analyze ourselves.

Moreover, a mobile device can have so many applications installed on it by different organizations that it is easy for third parties to get a deeper insight into our lifestyle, life pattern, and deep secrets, and take many different actions based on the key pointers gathered. There may be possibilities that not only benefit these third parties, but may also benefit us. They can try to make us aware of things that we were ignorant of as regards ourselves or suggest better ways to perform certain activities we do, thus improving our life overall. The possibilities are infinite and left to our imagination on how ML in mobile can be achieved and implemented.

We are also seeing an internet of things explosion. This is another dimension, where ML in mobile devices becomes key. The sensors sending out different information from time to time can be kept close to the sensor, rather than transmitting all the way to a server. Different protocols could be used to communicate between the sensors and mobile devices for such data exchange and timely actions could be taken swiftly. Here, again, the possibilities are innumerable, groundbreaking innovations are happening, and this is just the tip of the iceberg.

In this chapter, we are going to gain insights into the following topics:

- Key ML mobile applications
- Key innovation areas
- Opportunities for stakeholders—what are the key stakeholders in the mobile ML ecosystem doing?

Key ML mobile applications

In this section, we will look at some of the most popular mobile applications and understand what they are doing in the field of mobile ML.

Facebook

Facebook has developed an AI platform, Caffe2Go. Through this toolset, Facebook initially wanted to provide enriched AI and AR experiences to users. They are enabling users to process videos and images through on-device ML and perform certain tasks without having to transmit these videos and images to the backend for complex image and video processing. Their style transfer toolkit enables users to take the artistic qualities of one image style, and apply it to other images and videos.

Google Maps

Google has introduced TensorFlow Lite as well as ML Kit that enables users to perform mobile ML in mobile applications. Google Maps from Google is a classic example of ML on mobile.

Snapchat

Snapchat is innovating on complex ML algorithms that are able to perceive facial features on an image captured by the camera. These algorithms try to learn the facial features and then try to create a mask with key facial feature points. This mask can then be used to juxtapose with funny graphics to create images left to the imagination and creativity of users.

Tinder

Tinder, which was launched in 2012, is a social app that facilitates communication between mutually interested users. Users use a left or right swipe to choose photos of other users and potentially match with them. Tinder introduced a smart photos feature that increases users, ability to find a proper match, leveraging ML algorithms. This feature allows users to see the most famous photos first, as the underlying model is constantly learning and reordering the photographs by analyzing the swipe action behavior of the user.

Netflix

Netflix uses ML to provide quality streaming experiences to its users. Viewing streaming content in mobile devices is a lot more complicated than in other channels. Netflix is implementing complex ML algorithms to predict network bandwidth, caching requirements, and video adaptability requirements for devices based on content viewed in order to improve and enhance the streaming experience.

Oval Money

Oval Money uses ML algorithms to learn user spending patterns in order to suggest savings options to end users. It is able to recognize regular recurring patterns and identify duplicate payments to help users in saving money.

ImprompDo

ImprompDo is a time management application that learns user behavior and manages the to-do list. It prompts users at the best time they would be able to attend to their items in the to-do list, based on the knowledge it has gained by studying the user's behavior and their regular time schedule, the location they are in, and so on.

Dango

Dango is a emoji predictor application that suggests the perfect emoji for the context of the conversation. It uses learning algorithms to understand the different emotions and the context of the conversation to come up with timely emojis.

Carat

Carat monitors all activity happening on a mobile phone and provides suggestions to save battery power.

Uber

Uber uses ML techniques to help provide an estimated time of arrival and cost to riders. It also helps in providing detailed information and maps to the drivers to meet this estimated time of arrival.

GBoard

GBoard, Google's mobile keyboard for iOS and Android, uses ML to predict what the user is going to type before they actually type it.

Key innovation areas

The following sections detail some of the business areas where innovation is happening, leveraging the power of ML. A number of players are already leading the way in this regard.

Personalization applications

Understanding user behavior by leveraging various parameters that are provided through mobile devices and understanding their life patterns for the purposes of personalization will be of value to users. When the same mobile application is going to cater to user profiles across a broad spectrum, it will be of significant value if it could provide specific features that best suit the person using it. Such advanced personalization could be brought into applications by leveraging ML.

Healthcare

Here, there are various use cases that help track various health parameters that can be tracked, learned, and put into use for providing innovations in healthcare, such as diagnostic applications that can diagnose based on pictures and sound from mobile applications.

Fitness tracking and consumer healthcare applications that track the regular health and fitness data of individuals through mobile applications can prevent various lifestyle-related diseases.

These mobile applications could, in fact, change user behavior through alerts and notifications and make them take any action required by monitoring their lifestyle. They could, for example, suggest going for a walk, taking medication, and blinking an eye.

Targeted promotions and marketing

Mobile applications can be used to study user behavior and track user preferences to provide targeted promotions to users. Most user information collected, such as demographics, usage statistics, and profile information, can be analyzed using ML algorithms to make solid predictions on what products or services to promote for a particular person. So, in alignment with this, targeted marketing and advertisements could be aimed at users.

Visual and audio recognition

Mobile applications can identify circumstances and the user environment and modify the audio/video controls of the device, or play suitable audios and videos as per user preferences.

E-commerce

Mobile applications with ML intelligence can have various use cases in the e-commerce sector. One such example is indoor navigation applications in retail stores that improve business.

Indoor navigation deals with **navigation within buildings**. Because GPS reception is normally non-existent inside buildings, other positioning technologies are used here when automatic positioning is desired. Wi-Fi or beacons (**Bluetooth Low Energy (BLE)**) are often used in this case to create a so-called **indoor GPS**. Unlike GPS, however, they also enable you to determine the actual floor level. Most applications require an indoor routing functionality that guides people precisely through a building using an indoor navigation app and, in this way, automatically determines their position—very similar to the navigation systems that we use in our cars.

In many top e-commerce sites, product recommendations are provided when we purchase a certain product. This is done based on browsing history, purchase history, user query understanding, ranking, and user favorite determination, coupled with user situation, location, preferences, and constraints.

In e-commerce, trend prediction and taking immediate steps as per trends observed play a huge role in sales. The gaps between the two can largely be fixed by ML algorithms efficiently.

Finance management

ML is being used in every phase of finance management. User portfolio management, fraud detection, trading, loan management, and customer service are the different phases where combining user data and profiles could provide innumerable opportunities to service the customer differently and thereby leverage ML algorithms.

Gaming and entertainment

More realistic and engaging augmented virtual reality, combined with ML, could provide stunning personalized gaming and entertainment experiences to end users.

Content management, video streaming, and content rendering could be done more efficiently and in a more effective manner by leveraging various parameters, such as device capabilities, user preferences, and network capabilities, by applying ML.

Enterprise apps

Enterprise applications that had a lot of mundane repeatable activities have now been made interesting, and even more productive, with new insights that are available to enterprise staff, which could actually make the decisions better and more valuable to the enterprise, thereby saving the enterprise a significant amount of money.

The recruitment, time management, operation and capital expenditure, travel, and sales processes could be customized for specific users, clients, and geographies, leveraging the huge enterprise data available, and applying ML algorithms on them to come up with useful timely predictions.

Real estate

Powerful visualization software based on machine, neural networks, and augmented reality, when combined, could help the real estate sector significantly by enabling customers to visualize their dream home and model the home on the fly to suit their preferences.

IKEA has already introduced an application called **IKEA Place** (`https://itunes.apple.com/us/app/ikea-place/id1279244498?mt=8`) that enables users to visualize how the furniture they choose would fit into their homes.

Similarly, Azati's image modeling application enables users to replace the existing wall covering with other choices, thus enabling the user to view instantly their choice of covering on the model house they plan to buy or decorate.

Agriculture

There are various solutions that could be provided to farmers through mobile applications. The images of the soil and plants captured through the smartphone could be analyzed to provide useful insights on soil restoration techniques, tips for weeding, plant health control, and so on. These images could be analyzed on various parameters, such as soil defects, plant pests and diseases, defects, and nutrient deficiencies in soil. The possibilities are innumerable and could be extended to all steps in agriculture to help improve crop yield.

Energy

The energy sector is one sector where, if ML is applied, it could bring in lot of savings to energy spend, thereby protecting the environment and helping us go green.

Machine learning-enabled smart homes that can be controlled based on user preferences and availability, which could be tracked through mobile applications, can bring huge energy savings to each home.

Self-driving cars could also save energy by optimizing the routes and utilization of the same car by multiple people travelling the same route, regulating speed and energy spend at all times, and thereby saving fuel.

ML could also be used in the smart grid and its maintenance, where it could predict the point of failure and the time at which failure occurred, so the required preventive steps can be taken.

A smart grid is an electrical grid that includes a variety of operational and energy measures, including smart meters, smart appliances, renewable energy resources, and energy efficient resources. Electronic power conditioning and control of the production and distribution of electricity are important aspects of the smart grid. It is an electricity supply network that uses digital communications technology to detect and react to local changes in usage.

Mobile security

ML can be used for facial recognition tools that may be used for authentication and authorization of usage of applications in mobile devices.

Microsoft, Google, and others are working extensively in this area to secure their operating systems, as well as the mobile applications present in these OSes, from getting attacked by security threats.

Google has also rolled out an ML algorithm, called **peer group analysis**. This helps to identify harmful applications from the Google Play store, by tracking applications that unnecessarily collect or send data without any specific need.

Z9 software from Zimperium is an example of mobile device malware detection software that leverages ML to implement mobile security.

Opportunities for stakeholders

This section provides details of the key stakeholders in the landscape who contribute and determine the success and spread of ML on mobile devices. It explores how they contribute to mobile ML and what innovations are being carried out by each of them to increase the acceptance of mobile ML and make it reach far and wide.

Hardware manufacturers

The hardware is the platform that forms the basis for executing ML mobile applications. ML has specific requirements in terms of processing units and memory in order to run the complex ML algorithms. Until recently hardware limitations was one reason that drove the majority of ML processing to be undertaken in backend servers where there are no limits on processing units or memory. But now, most device manufacturers are making groundbreaking innovations that render hardware suitable for running mobile on-device ML applications:

- Apple has already designed and built a neural engine as part of its iPhone X's main chip set to handle complex ML-driven image processing.
- In the Pixel 2 device, Google has also built a custom chip set that caters to ML needs.
- Huawei's Mate 10 also has a neural network processing unit built into it.
- ARM has launched a project designed to create an AI-driven smart chip that will allow mobile devices to continue running ML algorithms even when offline. This will reduce data traffic, speed up processing, and also save battery power consumed.
- Qualcomm is also working with ARM to produce next generation mobile devices that enable ML algorithms to be run efficiently.

Mobile operating system vendors

Mobile operating systems such as iOS and Android, as well as Microsoft Windows mobile, are catering to the needs of running mobile ML algorithms on mobile devices. Various features has been incorporated into the operating system itself to support mobile ML.

Third-party mobile ML SDK providers

As we have seen in this book, there are various SDKs available that will help programmers create mobile ML programs:

- TensorFlow Lite
- Caffe2Go
- Core ML
- ML Kit
- Fritz

We have gone through the high-level architecture of these SDKs and also written sample mobile ML applications using each of the preceding SDKs in this book.

There are opportunities for all in the following areas of mobile ML technology enablement:

- Just like hybrid mobile application development, there can be way for hybrid ML model development that could employ a common language to develop these ML models
- There are many issues in terms of model deployment and upgrading of the deployed live ML models in the field
- There are many things to improve in terms of monitoring the performance and usage of the ML models in the field
- There is a lot of work to be undertaken to support many ML algorithms in these SDKs
- Now, predominantly, only prediction and usage of models is being done from mobile; training can also be undertaken from mobile on-device training enablement

ML mobile application developers

As mobile application developers, you have a huge opportunity in front of you to create groundbreaking and innovative solutions in this field. The possibilities are innumerable, and the implementation method is also simplified, as we have seen in the examples in this chapter. Being well versed in mobile application development, if you can get a basic idea of the ML algorithms, you can put them to use to solve critical problems and bring value-driven innovation to end users.

Summary

In this chapter, we learned about the future of ML in the field of mobile and how it will be useful to users. We also discussed different mobile applications that use ML, including Facebook, Netflix, and Google Maps.

We also saw how a variety of business areas are using ML applications and the various opportunities that exist for stakeholders in the field of ML using mobile.

Question and Answers

In this appendix, we will go through the concepts and points that could not be covered in the chapters, but that are essential to understand and appreciate mobile machine learning holistically. We will dwell on questions that may be on your mind and try to provide answers to those questions that are related to this domain.

FAQs

We will organize the FAQs into three basic sections:

- The first section will look into questions that are more generic in nature, related to data science, machine learning, and so on.
- The second section will look into specific questions related to the different mobile machine learning frameworks.
- The third and final section will look into specific questions related to mobile machine learning project implementation.

Data science

In this section, we will be answering a few questions related to data science and its uses.

What is data science?

Data science is the extraction of relevant insights from data. It is a culmination of many fields, such as mathematics, machine learning, computer programming, statistical modeling, data engineering and visualization, pattern recognition and learning, uncertainty modeling, data warehousing, and cloud computing. The skills required to pursue these fields include engineering, maths, science, statistics, programming, creativity and data keeping, and maintenance.

Where is data science used?

Data science is used in **Artificial Intelligence (AI)** and machine learning. It solves complex data problems to bring out insights that were unknown prior to applying it. It brings out unknown correlations between data that are extremely relevant and useful to a business.

What is big data?

Big data usually includes datasets with sizes beyond the ability of commonly used software tools to capture, manage, and handle them.

Big data is characterized by the three Vs, proposed by Gartner in 2001:

- **Volume**: The amount of data is enormous and increasing
- **Velocity**: The rate at which the data is accumulated is rapid and increasing
- **Variety**: The number of features/characteristics being captured is large and growing

 Gartner's 2012 definition reads: *Big data is high volume, high velocity, and/or high variety information assets that require new forms of processing to enable enhanced decision making, insight discovery and process optimization.*

Big data can comprise big data systems, big data analytics, and big datasets.

What is data mining?

Data mining is the process of examining large pre-existing datasets and extracting useful insights from them.

Relationship between data science and big data

Data science does not necessarily involve big data, but the fact that data is scaling up makes big data an important aspect of data science.

What are artificial neural networks?

Artificial neural networks (ANNs) are computing systems inspired by the biological neural networks that constitute animal brains. These systems are not programmed with a specific task rule, but perform tasks by considering examples without being programmed, for example, image recognition. To recognize a rose, it learns the characteristics of rose to define a sample as a rose, through learning and not through programming.

What is AI?

AI refers to the simulation of human brain functions by machines. This is achieved by creating an ANN that can show human intelligence. The primary human functions that an AI machine performs include logical reasoning, learning, and self-correction. This is a very complex field, and to make machines that are inherently not smart think and act like humans requires lot of computing power and data feeds.

AI is classified into two parts:

- **General AI**: Making machines smart in wide areas, similar to humans in thinking and reasoning. This has still not been achieved today and many ongoing research activities have already been initiated.
- **Narrow AI**: Making machines smart in specific areas, such as digit recognition and playing chess. This is possible today.

How are data science, AI, and machine learning interrelated?

This is an interesting and important piece of information to know, as to how exactly data science, AI, and machine learning are related to each other:

- **AI**: This area is trying to mimic human intelligence artificially. Just as humans are able to see, observe the data around them, and take decisions, the same is being tried through machines. It is a very wide area. The technology is still evolving. And to achieve a small task that a human does very easily through AI, a humongous amount of data is required.
- **Machine learning**: Subset of AI. Narrow focus on specific problem areas. The technology has implementations for real-life use cases. It is the connecting bridge between AI and data science.

- **Data science**: It is a field of data study and extracting information from it. This can use machine learning to analyze data, big data, and so on:

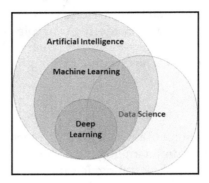

Machine learning framework

In this section, we will look at a few of the machine learning frameworks we have already gone through in the book, and the ones we have not gone through as well, and just give a few pointers on them.

Caffe2

- Caffe2 from Facebook is one of the key mobile machine learning frameworks that was not discussed in this book. More details can be obtained from `https://caffe2.ai/`.
- Caffe2 is a deep learning framework that provides an easy and straightforward way to experiment with deep learning and leverage community contributions of new models and algorithms.
- The original Caffe framework was useful for large-scale product use cases, especially with its unparalleled performance and well-tested C++ code base.
- Caffe2 is an improvement over the original Caffe framework in a number of features.
- It has got a steep learning curve to understand and to start coding examples using the framework.

scikit-learn

- Scikit-learn is one of the best known machine learning package and provides efficient implementation versions of a large number of common machine learning algorithms.
- It is NOT a mobile machine learning package. However, models created using scikit-learn can be converted to Core ML and TensorFlow Lite models using conversion tools, and used in mobile applications directly.
- It has got similar and uniform API implementations across machine learning algorithms and very comprehensive supportive documentation.
- It is very easy to learn scikit-learn and implement and extend models using it.
- Scikit-learn was initially developed by David Cournapeau as a Google Summer of Code project in 2007. Later, Matthieu Brucher joined the project and started to use it as part of his thesis work. In 2010, INRIA got involved and the first public release (v 0.1 beta) was published in late January 2010. The project now has more than 30 active contributors and has had paid sponsorship from INRIA, Google, Tinyclues, and the Python Software Foundation.
- Scikit-learn provides a range of supervised and unsupervised learning algorithms via a consistent interface in Python.
- It is licensed under a permissive simplified BSD license and is distributed under many Linux distributions, encouraging academic and commercial use.
- The library is built upon SciPy, which must be installed before you can use scikit-learn.

TensorFlow

- TensorFlow is an open source library for fast numerical computing. It was created and is maintained by Google, and released under the Apache 2.0 open source license. The API is in the Python programming language, although there is access to the underlying C++ API.
- There is a separate flavor for mobile, which we already went through in detail and used in our practical hands-on exercises in this book.
- Models created in TensorFlow can be used and converted to models for TensorFlow for mobile and TensorFlow Lite, and used in mobile applications.

- TensorFlow was designed for use both in research and development and in production systems. It can run on single CPU systems and GPUs, as well as mobile devices and large-scale distributed systems of hundreds of machines.
- Mathematically, a tensor is an n-dimensional vector. It can be used to represent n-dimensional datasets. Flow refers to a graph; the graph can never be cyclic and each node in the graph represents an operation such as addition, subtraction, and so on. And each operation results in the formation of a new tensor.
- Tensor flow enables the evaluation of each node in parallel and not hence the idle waster time waiting for a node evaluation like in serial mode is eliminated by TensorFlow.
- TensorFlow allows users to make use of parallel computing devices to perform operations faster.

Core ML

- Apple released Core ML at WWDC'17, and it was updated to Core ML 2 this year. As a reminder, Core ML enables developers to integrate machine learning models into iOS and MacOS apps. This was the first big attempt in this field, and initially developers really liked it for several reasons.
- Core ML supports a variety of machine learning models, including neural networks, tree ensembles, support vector machines, and generalized linear models. Core ML requires the Core ML model format (models with a `.mlmodel` file extension).
- Apple also provides converters to convert the models created in several other libraries to Core ML format. As we have used these converters in this book, we find that these converters are extremely simple to use and work with most famous existing machine learning libraries.
- Apple also provides several popular, open source models that are already in the Core ML model format, which can be directly downloaded and used in building our applications.
- Core ML is optimized for on-device performance, which minimizes memory footprint and power consumption. Running strictly on the device also ensures that user data is kept secure, and the app runs even in the absence of a network connection.
- Core ML's biggest advantage is that it is extremely simple to use. Just a few lines of code can help you integrate a complete machine learning model. Since the release of Core ML, there has been a flood of innovative projects using it. However, there are limitations around what Core ML can do.

- Core ML can only help you integrate pre-trained ML models into your app. So, this means you can do predictions only; no model training is possible.
- Thus far, Core ML has proved to be extremely useful for developers. Core ML 2, which was announced at WWDC this year, should improve inference time by 30% using techniques called **quantization** and **batch prediction**.

Mobile machine learning project implementation

In this section, we will go through the basic questions that any machine learning project implementer would have in mind before embarking on the project.

What are the high-level important items to be considered before starting the project?

The following are the high-level items that need to be addressed before starting the project:

- Clear definition of problem as per the ML definition we have seen, with clear inputs for task T, performance measure P, and experience E
- Data availability with the required volume
- Design decision for on-mobile or cloud-based mobile machine learning framework
- Proper selection of machine learning framework that suits our requirements

What are the roles and skills required to implement a mobile machine learning project?

The following skills and roles can be planned for the mobile machine learning project:

- **Domain expert/specialist**: Provides input on problem, data, features in data, business context, and so on
- **Machine learning data scientist**: Analyzes the data, does feature engineering and data preprocessing, and builds the machine learning model
- **Mobile application developer**: Utilizes the mobile machine learning model to build the mobile application
- **Tester**: Tests the model as well as the mobile application

Here, each role can be learned by others through this book and can be performed by single or multiple people for successful implementation of the mobile machine learning project.

What should you focus on when testing the mobile machine learning project?

The key thing to be tested in the project is the mobile machine learning model. So, independent of the mobile application, the model needs to be tested thoroughly.

We have already seen what things should be focused on while testing the machine learning model. The training data, test data, and cross-validation need to be considered while testing the model. The performance measure of the chosen model to be measured. For each run of the clear record keeping of the results to be done, so that we clearly know for a delta change in feature set of the input data, what is the delta change in output. All the concepts explained in Chapter 1, *Introduction to Machine Learning on Mobile*, related to accuracy, precision, recall, error, and so on should be understood clearly by an engineer testing machine learning models. Also, for each type of algorithm, the error and performance measure metrics vary, which should be taken into due consideration while testing the models. Testing machine learning models is itself worth a book and dwelling on the details in this book is out of scope.

What is the help that the domain expert will provide to the machine learning project?

The domain expert/specialist is a key role for the success of any machine learning project and his specific value will be in the following areas:

- Definition of problem statement and help in correctly understanding the expectations of the solution
- Data preparation:
    - What are good candidates to be selected in feature engineering and kept as predictor attributes?
    - How to combine multiple objectives/attributes that would help solve the problem statement
    - How to sample to select the test set and training set
    - Help in data cleaning

- Progress monitoring and result interpretation:
    - Defining the accuracy of prediction required
    - Determining if more data/additional data is required, based on the progress made
    - Making a checkpoint in between and determine if the progress made is in alignment with the problem statement defined and the solution pursued is in line and can be further pursued in same lines or there is need to take a different path/re calibrate methods
- Continuous update and feedback on progress

What are the common pitfalls in machine learning projects?

The following are some of the common pitfalls seen in any machine learning project:

- Unrealistic objectives, unclear problem definition with no proper objectives
- Data problems:
    - Insufficient data to establish predictive patterns
    - Incorrect selection of predictor attributes
    - Data preparation problems
    - Data normalization problems—failure to normalize data across datasets
    - Bias in data use to solve the problem
- Inappropriate machine learning method selection:
    - The ML method selected doesn't suit the problem statement defined
    - Not trying alternative algorithms
- Giving up too soon. This happens very often. Engineers tend to lose interest if they don't see initial results and are unable to do the various permutations and combinations of various dependent factors, and also do systematic book keeping for the results. If pursued continuously/methodically with proper record keeping and trying out the various possibilities, machine learning problems can be easily solved.

Installation

In this section, we will go through the different installation procedures required for setting up the tools and SDKs used to create the programs in this book.

Python

In this book, we worked with Python to create the ML models. So, you must know how to install Python in your system to go through the practical examples.

Go to `https://www.python.org/downloads/`.

It will show you the latest version to download; download the installer and install it.

While installing in Windows, it will ask whether to add Python to the path environment variable. Check the box to do that automatically for yours. Otherwise, you need to add it to your path variable manually.

To check whether Python is installed on your machine or not, go to Command Prompt or a Terminal and type `python`. It should show the Python prompt. Otherwise, you need to set the path variable if you already installed it to your drive.

Python dependencies

Python will come with the `pip` package manager by default. You can install using `pip`. The syntax is as follows:

```
pip install package name
```

For more information on available packages, you can visit `https://pypi.org/project/pip/`. In this book, we have given all the dependency installation commands in their respective chapters.

Xcode

First, create a developer account in Apple and log in to your account at `https://developer.apple.com/`. Click on **Downloads** and scroll down/search for the latest Xcode, above 9.4, and then click it to download. It will download the XZIP file. Extract it and install in your Mac machine by dragging it into your applications folder.

References

The following are a few of the references you can follow to learn more about machine learning on mobile:

- **Machine Learning Mastery**: https://machinelearningmastery.com/
- **Analytics Vidhya**: https://www.analyticsvidhya.com/
- **Fritz**: https://fritz.ai/
- **ML Kit**: https://developers.google.com/ml-kit/
- **TensorFlow Lite**: https://www.tensorflow.org/lite/
- **Core ML**: https://developer.apple.com/documentation/coreml?changes=_8
- **Caffe2**: https://caffe2.ai/

Other Books You May Enjoy

If you enjoyed this book, you may be interested in these other books by Packt:

Machine Learning Projects for Mobile Applications
Karthikeyan NG

ISBN: 9781788994590

- Demystify the machine learning landscape on mobile
- Age and gender detection using TensorFlow Lite and Core ML
- Use ML Kit for Firebase for in-text detection, face detection, and barcode scanning
- Create a digit classifier using adversarial learning
- Build a cross-platform application with face filters using OpenCV
- Classify food using deep CNNs and TensorFlow Lite on iOS

Machine Learning with Core ML
Joshua Newnham

ISBN: 9781788838290

- Understand components of an ML project using algorithms, problems, and data
- Master Core ML by obtaining and importing machine learning model, and generate classes
- Prepare data for machine learning model and interpret results for optimized solutions
- Create and optimize custom layers for unsupported layers
- Apply CoreML to image and video data using CNN
- Learn the qualities of RNN to recognize sketches, and augment drawing
- Use Core ML transfer learning to execute style transfer on images

Leave a review - let other readers know what you think

Please share your thoughts on this book with others by leaving a review on the site that you bought it from. If you purchased the book from Amazon, please leave us an honest review on this book's Amazon page. This is vital so that other potential readers can see and use your unbiased opinion to make purchasing decisions, we can understand what our customers think about our products, and our authors can see your feedback on the title that they have worked with Packt to create. It will only take a few minutes of your time, but is valuable to other potential customers, our authors, and Packt. Thank you!

Index

hyperplane 96

I

IKEA Pace
  reference 231
ImprompDo 227
indoor navigation 229
innovation areas
  about 228
  agriculture 231
  e-commerce 229
  energy 232
  enterprise apps 231
  finance management 230
  gaming and entertainment 230
  healthcare 229
  mobile security 232
  personalization applications 228
  real estate 231
  targeted promotions and marketing 229
  visual and audio recognition 229
installations
  about 246
  Python 246
  Python dependencies 246
  Xcode 246
internet of things (IOT) 7
Inverse Document Frequency (IDF) 136
iOS Mobile application
  writing 199

K

Keras model
  building, with sequential API 208
Keras
  about 201
  installing 201
  reference 201
  uses 201
Kernel Trick 138

L

landmark 125
learning
  challenges 24

reinforcement learning 23
semi-supervised learning 22
supervised learning 18, 20
types 18
unsupervised learning 20
linear regression
  about 47, 97
  dataset 97
  dataset naming 97, 100
Linear SVM algorithm
  about 137
  used, for problem solving in Core ML 139
logistic regression 48

M

machine learning framework
  about 240
  Caffe2 240
  Core ML 242
  scikit-learn 241
  TensorFlow 241
machine learning
  applying 8
  defining 9
  implementing, in mobile application 26
  inference process, on server 33
  issue, defining 12
  mobile tools 35
  model, building 15
  model, training 29
  on mobile, advantages 24
  predictions, deploying 18
  process 11
  process, on device 33, 34
  process, on server 33
  relationship, with data science 239
  SDKs 35
  service providers, utilizing 27, 29
  training, on desktop 30, 32
  training, on device 33
  using, on mobile devices 24
  using, scenarios 10
market-basket analysis 59
maximum-margin classifier 49
maximum-margin hyperplane 49

www.ingramcontent.com/pod-product-compliance
Lightning Source LLC
Chambersburg PA
CBHW080633060326
40690CB00021B/4911